ALL THIS, AND HEAVEN TOO

KALOS

The word *kalos* (καλός) means beautiful. It is the call of the good; that which arouses interest, desire: "I am here." Beauty brings the appetite to rest at the same time as it wakens the mind from its daily slumber, calling us to look afresh at that which is before our very eyes. It makes virgins of us all, and of everything—there, before us, lies something that we never noticed before. Beauty consists in *integritas sive perfectio* (integrity and perfection) and *claritas* (brightness/clarity). It is the reason why we rise and why we sleep—that great night of dependence, one that reveals the borrowed existence of all things, if, that is, there is to be a thing at all, or if there is to be a person at all. Here lies the ground of all science, of philosophy, and of all theology, indeed, of our each and every day.

This series will seek to provide intelligent-yet-accessible volumes that have the innocence of beauty and of true adventure, and in so doing remind us all again of that which we took for granted, most of all thought itself.

SERIES EDITORS:
Conor Cunningham, Eric Austin Lee, and Joseph Terry

All This, and Heaven Too

A GUIDE FOR ALL SOULS

...

Caitlin Smith Gilson

With original art and contributions by
Carol Scott

Foreword by
Daniel Fitzpatrick

CASCADE *Books* · Eugene, Oregon

ALL THIS, AND HEAVEN TOO
A Guide for All Souls

Copyright © 2024 Caitlin Smith Gilson. Artwork copyright © 2024 Carol Scott. All rights reserved. Except for brief quotations in critical publications or reviews, no part of this book may be reproduced in any manner without prior written permission from the publisher. Write: Permissions, Wipf and Stock Publishers, 199 W. 8th Ave., Suite 3, Eugene, OR 97401.

Cascade Books
An Imprint of Wipf and Stock Publishers
199 W. 8th Ave., Suite 3
Eugene, OR 97401

www.wipfandstock.com

PAPERBACK ISBN: 979-8-3852-1411-2
HARDCOVER ISBN: 979-8-3852-1412-9
EBOOK ISBN: 979-8-3852-1413-6

Cataloguing-in-Publication data:

Names: Smith Gilson, Caitlin [author]. | Scott, Carol [artist].

Title: All this, and heaven too : a guide for all souls / Caitlin Smith Gilson ; with original artwork by Carol Scott.

Description: Eugene, OR: Cascade Books, 2024 | Series: Kalos | Includes bibliographical references and index.

Identifiers: ISBN 979-8-3852-1411-2 (paperback) | ISBN 979-8-3852-1412-9 (hardcover) | ISBN 979-8-3852-1413-6 (ebook)

Subjects: LCSH: Future life—Christianity. | Heaven—Christianity. | Eschatology. | Hope—Religious aspects—Christianity. | Death—Religious aspects—Christianity. | Christian poetry, American. | Artwork.

Classification: BT846.2 S658 2024 (print) | BT846.2 (ebook)

Cover art, *God of the Cosmos*, by Carol Scott. All poetry comes from Carol Scott and Caitlin Smith Gilson, *Heaven Sent: The Passion of the Last Words*. Kalos. Eugene, OR: Cascade, forthcoming 2025.

Grateful to Mark Surber for his superb cover design.

For my Fred and our beautiful, beautiful,
brilliant daughters, now grown.

My children
Every essence of all the good
Packed in fragrance
I could be shot through with mortal arrow
It could pierce my heart
Rip my bones apart
And I would be everything
Everything that happiness is and should be
Loving them

For Cyril—this work of love would not have come into being without your friendship.

For Pam—We will always have our Josh and Daisi at play under Grace.

Baroque Rosary. Art by Carol Scott

Contents

Crystal and Coke. Art by Carol Scott x
Foreword by Daniel Fitzpatrick xi
Full Throttle. Art by Carol Scott xiv
Acknowledgments xv
Note on Art xvii
Luminous Mysteries. Art by Carol Scott xviii

PART I: THE HOPE FOR HEAVEN
 St. Joseph's Day Altar. Art by Carol Scott
 "New Life." Poem by Carol Scott & Caitlin Smith Gilson

1. Up Close to Death: The Uninvited Guest 5
 Vanitas. Art by Carol Scott
 "In the Final Month." Poem by Caitlin Smith Gilson

2. Within Every Question Is a Conversation with God 9
 Pirogue in the Sun. Art by Carol Scott
 "If You Could See Me." Poem by Carol Scott & Caitlin Smith Gilson

3. What Happens to Us When We Make Ourselves a Gift to the Person Who Now Has Died? 16
 The Empty Bed. Art by Carol Scott
 "What Can I Say about Loving You?" Poem by Carol Scott & Caitlin Smith Gilson

4. Heaven Misplaced: Recovered through Christ 22
 Contemplation. Art by Carol Scott
 "You Have Taken My Child," poem by Caitlin Smith Gilson

5. There Are Layers upon Layers of Grief 27
 Dance Ballerina Dance. Art by Carol Scott
 "I Could have Perished in My Sorrow." Poem by Caitlin Smith Gilson

CONTENTS

6. The Hunt for Heaven: The Tale Underneath All Tales 34
    Flying to Infinity and Beyond. Art by Carol Scott
    "We are Swimming between Universes." Poem by Carol Scott & Caitlin Smith Gilson

7. Do We Lack and Long in Heaven without Our Bodies? 43
    St. Teresa in Ecstasy. Art by Carol Scott
    "Split Apart." Poem by Caitlin Smith Gilson

8. How Are Humans (for Once) Higher Than Angels? 50
    City Park with the Girls. Art by Carol Scott
    "The One Who Shares My Heart Can Make Anything." Poem by Caitlin Smith Gilson

9. What Can We Understand of Heaven for Souls Separated from Their Bodies? 56
    Split Apart. Art by Carol Scott
    "Today When I Left." Poem by Carol Scott & Caitlin Smith Gilson

10. No Man Is an Island: What Human Experience Teaches Us about Heaven 63
    Gods and Fates. Art by Carol Scott
    "When You Sway the Heavens." Poem by Caitlin Smith Gilson

11. A Glimpse of Hell: The Conscience of Failed Love 73
    St. Paul's Moment. Art by Carol Scott
    "My Father." Poem by Caitlin Smith Gilson

12. What Can We Say about the Experience/Non-Experience of Death? 92
    Lost Time. Art by Carol Scott
    "You are Constellation." Poem by Carol Scott & Caitlin Smith Gilson

PART II: WHAT IS THE RESURRECTED STATE LIKE?
    Spirit of Our Lady of Holy Cross. Art by Carol Scott
    "On the Train." Poem by Caitlin Smith Gilson

13. Our Five Senses: Signposts of the Resurrected State and Our Fallenness 110
    Light Sauce. Art by Carol Scott
    "The Wordless Said." Poem by Carol Scott & Caitlin Smith Gilson

14. Stairway to Heaven: What Does Christ Tell Us about the Resurrected State? 131
> *Redolent Blue.* Art by Carol Scott
> "Goodnight Love Maker." Poem by Carol Scott & Caitlin Smith Gilson

15. Christ Enters into Us: This Is the Key to Our Glorified Body 138
> *Magnum Opus.* Art by Carol Scott
> "The Passing Thought." Poem by Caitlin Smith Gilson

16. Lovers in Paradise: What Becomes of Friendships, Fellowships, Marriages 148
> *The Lovers.* Art by Carol Scott
> "The Friendship in Christ." Poem by Caitlin Smith Gilson

17. Closing Miscellany: Play, Laughter, and Animals 165
> *Susie Mermaid.* Art by Carol Scott
> "Of Love and God." Poem by Caitlin Smith Gilson
> *The Guardian Angels.* Art by Carol Scott
> "On the Way." Poem by Caitlin Smith Gilson

Bibliography 179
Index 185

Crystal and Coke. Art by Carol Scott

Foreword

by Daniel Fitzpatrick

Summer, as I write, is passing away. Slowly this side of the earth is shouldering away from the sun, and among the many partings of the past months, one of the harshest has been the death of my cousin. Still in his late twenties, he succumbed, after two years' struggle, to a rare cancer. The same friends and family members who had gathered six months before at his wedding, hoisting him aloft in the joy of the dance, gathered once again at his funeral, praying for his soul, weeping with his parents, leaning for a moment to toss a flower at the foot of his tomb or touch the warm stone of it in farewell. Summer is passing away, and my cousin's wife will soon face her first anniversary, already a widow.

Tragedy is present throughout the pages of this book. Whether in her searing meditations on the death of her niece Daisy or in her deft use of Eugene O'Neill's Tyrone family, Caitlin Smith Gilson invites, demands, allows our grief. Sin will have its wages, and, being paid this way, we are left so often to mourn our friends, our children, our parents, and above all ourselves.

And yet our mourning need not last forever. For death itself has suffered death at the wounded hands of the Christ, and Gilson's invitation to mourn is at the same time an invitation to rejoice in the renewed recognition that death is not the end but rather the point of intensified engagement with the life we have led to its doors. Heaven invites the soul moment by moment, and one of the tasks of the Christian is to learn once more to see the impress of heaven upon the earth and to let ourselves begin again to imagine what heaven might mean.

In his novel *The Moviegoer*, Walker Percy's protagonist, Binx Bolling, notes, as Percy often did, the difficulty we have in grappling with the questions of real import. As Binx observes, 98 percent of people believe in God and 2 percent are atheists, leaving exactly 0 percentage left over for the seeker. The figures themselves might apply better to the 1950s of the novel than to our own day, but the point remains the same: for many of us, describing ourselves as believers or atheists, Catholics or Presbyterians or Unitarians, is effectively a means of bracketing the questions, of assuming a ready-made attitude toward the transcendent so that we can go about the day-to-day business of life without the weight of wonder bearing down upon us.

All This, and Heaven Too, in something like Percy's vein, presents philosophy at its best, as a renewed encounter with truth which sparks our wonder and a fresh glimpse of beauty which commands us, "You must change your life." Gilson drives us again and again to question the suppositions by which we surrender our attitudes to the divine and the platitudes in which we seek a momentary anodyne to the way we feel as the strange beings we are, as humans inseparably body and soul subjected to precisely such separation in consequence of our own turning away from ourselves in turning away from God and from each other.

As Gilson remarks, "For years I had the uneasy sense that the way we viewed heaven short-circuited our faith. Our personal exercise of faith leads us to this short-sighted view. Thoughts of heaven cause a subterranean terror preventing any real and prolonged contemplation. My own thoughts participated in this reduction. I had a faith short-circuited by a notion of paradise that vacillated among a comic book understanding, a vacant phrasebook expressionism, and a half-terrified desire for something truer than I would ever dare to envision." For those of us raised in the age of television, heaven perhaps most readily conjures visions of white-robed, eagle-winged angels harping away eternity in the clouds. This is the good place, the better place, the place we mention as we pat a mourning shoulder or recall an aged aunt at a family Christmas party. It is the place we imagine when we don't want to imagine too hard, for committing ourselves to a heaven commensurate with the capacities of our souls and the gifts of God the Father means taking up the burden of wonder. It means coming to terms with the cross and the resurrection and the conviction that our bodies will indeed be restored to us. And there is terror in this, the terror "of the rumor of a knocking in a tomb," as Melville put it, the terror of that call, "Lazarus, come out," the terror of the empty grave.

The terror of heaven is the terror of the universe with no exit. Within its limitless confines, all our relationships bear undying meaning, such that the death of the beloved friend or bitter enemy is not the end of the matter. We go on—the parent of the dead child, the honeymoon widow, the wounded soldier—bearing our loss onward to a future that ineluctably means our own being lost to those we leave behind on earth, just as it means our being brought finally into that attitude to God, and to each other, shadowed forth in all our earthly acting.

What Gilson above all makes clear to the reader, contrary to the custom of our thinking, is that heaven and hell are not simply fairy worlds we might or might not meet beyond the veil of death. Rather, heaven and hell begin in the postures we daily assume with respect to the God who is always present to us. To set heaven wholly in the future is, as it were, to miss the point. For heaven, as St. Augustine recalls near the end of his *Confessions*, is nothing but the presence of God, a presence to which it is the task of our lives to begin to attend, if only darkly, as in a glass.

Nor can the heaven into which the Christ ascended be a mere spirit realm. As he went, Christ drew with him space and time, the body and the senses and the imagination, all that makes us human, into the life of God. Gilson reminds us at every turn that heaven will in the end be not a realm of separation but of ultimate intensity, the world where God will be all in all and where our whole being, body and soul, passions and affections and senses and appetites, will enter upon a pitch of being opened to us by the incarnation, passion, and resurrection of Christ. And the text, inviting us to this feast, is itself a feast for the senses. Whether in the astonishing paintings by Carol Scott, the heart-rending collaborative poetry of Scott and Gilson, or the dizzying array of artists, authors, and saints upon whose wisdom Gilson has drawn, we find ourselves in these pages all awash in the manifold goodness of the created order, attuned anew to the goodness for which we ourselves are made.

Gilson has here gone with Dante into the realm toward which we are ordered. In doing so, she has reminded us, with Dante, that it is not a realm strictly separable from our own. At every moment, Penelope-like, we are weaving or unweaving the two, time and eternity, heaven (or hell) and earth. Faced as we are with death, it can often feel too painful to carry on, to bear with us toward our own death the death we have encountered, to hold up hope in the midst of hopelessness, to borrow once more from Melville. Yet we press on to the end, assured by the God who has gone before us on the way, that the ache we call grief is no false promise, that the universe concludes not in tragedy but abides in the comic mastery of God.

Full Throttle. Art by Carol Scott

Acknowledgments

Many thanks to the marvelous editorial team at Wipf & Stock. Most particularly, Michael Thomson, Matthew Wimer, Zechariah Mickel, the remarkable Heather Carraher, Conor Cunningham, Eric Austin Lee, and Christopher Ben Simpson, and most especially Robin Parry, our brilliant and generous editor. Robin—your guidance and wisdom over the last few years have helped bring out the best in my work. I am blessed.

To Carol for all your invaluable guidance, magnificent artistry, and joyous passion for creation and beauty. I am especially grateful for your friendship. And to Susie our dear friend on the next writing adventure.

To Fr. Labastida, Mike, Susan, Irina, Ashlinn, Connie Christian, Bobby, Grace, Danny, Grace Gallaher, Aunt Nancy, Maria, Joseph Terry, Nicole, Todd, Philippe, Mark, Elizabeth, Erika, Victoria, and Cindy for all your love and support.

I am grateful to Daniel Fitzpatrick, for his brilliance, friendship, and generosity writing the foreword to this book.

Note on Art

All art in this volume is conceived and created by Gallery 600 Julia artist, Carol Scott. Carol is professor emeritus of art at the University of Holy Cross, New Orleans. She has had numerous one-person shows, has over six hundred artworks created, has exhibited in galleries, museums, won awards, and is collected and commissioned nationally and internationally. She has been honored with a one-person show in New York City and a retrospective in New Orleans at THE BUILDING Arts Venue & Gallery (www.building1427.com). The City of New Orleans selected her work for their permanent collection, and she has served as the vice president of the Women's Caucus for Art.

Carol also co-authored two books of poetry and art with Caitlin Smith Gilson, *Rhapsody and Redolence: The Crystal Decade* (Cascade, 2024) and *Luminous Darkness: The Passion of the Last Words* (Cascade, 2025). Carol's work has also been selected for the prestigious Chianciano Biennale in Tuscany for leading international and contemporary artists. To see her work visit Gallery 600 Julia in the Arts District of New Orleans (www.gallery600julia.com/carol-scott) and her website (www.carolscottart.com).

> When I saw Carol Scott's paintings, my first impression was their wondrous intensity—bursting with joy! The colors are shockingly bold, and the things in the painting feel like they are in motion. For me, her art expresses both movement and stillness, almost shouting with gladness. Because of its subject matter—I am thinking here specifically of "Luminous Mysteries," but all her works have this element—her art shimmers with profundity, as Scott seems to have penetrated into the deepest energy and passion that pours forth from Christ's cross. I can't think of other artists whose works pulsate with the joy and energy of being, and with the "pouring forth" or shouting with joy of sheer grace, that I find in Scott's best paintings, of which there are many.
>
> —Matthew Levering, James N. Jr. and Mary D. Perry Chair of Theology, University of Saint Mary of the Lake, IL; editor, *Word on Fire: The New Ressourcement Journal*

Luminous Mysteries. Art by Carol Scott

PART I

The Hope for Heaven

St. Joseph's Day Altar, by Carol Scott

You have been on my mind, I watch the light reflect on the water and I think of you
In a few hours nature changes, the tidewater governs my legs
And I think of you coming upon me, your body over mine, bestriding magnificence
What I know is that I never want you out of my mind
I want to think of you when the water feels like silk, when the waves die down
When the sun is at its last peak, before it dips into night
Your lips enthralling me, thinking now of what I can kiss, the wetness of my mouth
All your sides bathed in mine when the sun is at its last peak, when it dies down
Undercover, dripping diamonds
Pink striations, orange bands across the sky
You have been on mind all day, all night
New bold gold, old is over, peaked magnum of magic, naked music
Free form holding, pure touches, perfect fingers and hands
Sempre on my mind, always burning in memory

—"New Life," by Carol Scott & Caitlin Smith Gilson

As the deer pants for water, so I long for you, O God. I thirst for God, the living God. Where can I find him to come and stand before him?

—Psalm 42

1

Up Close to Death

The Uninvited Guest

Vanitas, by Carol Scott

All This, and Heaven Too

We never quite feel the satellites puncture the atmosphere
Rings of violent steam descending into the Atlantic
Defeated without playing any game, nor do we know
The dying of deep-rooted things, vines as thick as wheels of fate cut down
There are gallons of vacant expression untouched by feeling
Poured alongside our every walk
Trenches of ice, fueled with prehistoric death, careening towards the basic element
We navigate little with little, the crust of bread, the bitter types of ends consume us
Somewhere I am paddling up the waterfall that are my bones
Turning against their blood into the wilderness of breathing
There is a world rocking itself into oblivion, miles of souls shelved and waiting
Lost below the earth
Tell me, love, this is not for us
I cannot feel a time before my blood was warm, before blood was shed
Before altars and sacrifice
All of me, whatever I am is yours
There are deserts of dead planets circling us, yet they fit inside a single thought
This complexion of moving things, it will be the death of us
Still all of you, you are the glimpse
There is so much to this life, there are so few words we have, so few
But I tell you, love
In the final month of the year
Loving you has been the gift

   —"In the Final Month," by Caitlin Smith Gilson

SOMETHING ALWAYS HAPPENS—AN IMAGE, a moment, a terror, present one second, escaped the next—and we find ourselves thrust upon the sword of our own creeping mortality. This sharpened clarity occurred to me one evening as my father's legs gave out. They buckled underneath, balletic and violent against himself and his being. His spirit submitted to the law of gravity. His lifeforce was willed to the material floor by an unseen power too close and too universal to differentiate from the scenery. The heavy materiality that refused to act as his body further refused the soul, once its great friend, its walking stick and guide.

I gasped at this presence, at this sheer power that dressed me down and revealed my unpreparedness for the eternal things, for the little things, for the dappled things. We had been prepared that my father was declining and nearing more active death. Everything prepared us: the hospitalizations, the body wasting, the breathlessness, dementia, fear, fear of night, of hospital beds and long antiseptic corridors of loneliness. Surrounding us were wild ancient memories cut with the fine teeth of recollected childhood, some real, some fantastic, mixed with failed loves, regret, and the heart-aching need to square the circle. Above all, my father desired to achieve the harmony within the family intimacies that had perennially and rudely escaped such things, and would likely do so after his death.

My father's head fell back like that of an infant whose neck hadn't the strength to provide the needed support. He became another kind of pieta now softened into flesh. His eyes, which for days moved back and forth across the room speaking for him in his muteness, had rolled up into his head, producing in me such inadequacy and the unreadiness to relinquish him. Then, the exacting, ever exacting, and vitiating moment where death made its presence ferociously known. It had arrived. His mouth opened as if to gasp, wider though weaker in appearance. A dull cavernous space half-mouthing in silence. Everything, all sums, the geometry of expectation settled into a more secret calculation. Everything I am brought to the forefront: my littleness in the face of the universe, all felt presence and absence, every sensation dilated and restricted. As if a sky that had never been punctuated with the lights of civilization had recovered within his mouth its dark pitch and stars. All things that I was and ever will be were placed within his gaze. The sum of the realities that always elude capture pulled me with him to my knees onto the floor. Do I even know what is meant by "only say the Word..."?

There I was, without knowledge or wisdom, looking for the unsaid word on his lips. This is the word that could undo this death sentence surely and irremediably placed upon all my line, on every family line, and every living thing, on my husband, on my dear little ones. To know and not know all the same, this is what death does to us. This sentence is on my children, full of life and promise, born with imagined endless possibilities. This death sentences is on them even as they are bathed in heated waves of anticipation, hope, and futurity. How is it that my children were born with gleaming sunbeams in every crevice of their soft faces, and still the secret passenger has found its way into them before they were born? The pain of birth has from the outset already pronounced its final sentence. My father was once this child, an unrepeatable moment of wave upon wave, and light upon light. My father was once a little dreaming face calling forth seas as deep as memory, calling forth infinite promise upon promise. My father slack jawed and almost past knowing and being. We wait for death:

> Weave a circle round him thrice,
> And close your eyes with holy dread.
>
> —Samuel Taylor Coleridge, *Kubla Kahn*

Should death be personified, this fellow would likely give a wry smile. This is not to make light of the situation. Nothing dulls his element of surprise. There are more trapped doors, hidden passageways, secret languages he can navigate to make his presence felt again and again with the power of the first time. Our friend, dear Death, from the beginning has such tricks up his sleeves. Death has such ways to shock, to become the unexpected guest even and especially as he is waited for and upon. The guest of honor is running late, everyone has arrived, the doors are locked, the windows battened down. We are watching every corner for potential breeches, but still, Death finds a way to enter the festivities when least expected. Our dear friend has simply come to remind us that we cannot prepare ourselves for what prices must be paid from now to the grave.

2

Within Every Question Is a Conversation with God

Pirogue in the Sun, by Carol Scott

All This, and Heaven Too

If you could see me wrapped in a towel as orange as risen sun, hair wet
Body tired, wondering where you are, if you could see me
Curled in its companion sheet, resting in the few moments before life
Jotting lines, things are brighter than fresh squeezed juice, I have yet to hear the bells
Mark the time, this day must begin, I wonder where you are, I think of you in the depth
Within the silent parade of night, passing over and through, I am cut with electric color
Somewhere you sleep in the cool black of dark and shadow
Healing your body, resting your soul
Perhaps a shooting star passed your way? Perhaps an animal howled for you?
Rest is good, work is good, love is best, different places
Even time not the same, routine unshared . . .
At midday I wondered about you and walked into time
Perhaps the sun has passed your way? Perhaps the rain too? . . .
Today I touched a wall formed before Christ was born, hidden in the basement of a library
Too many faces lost, I placed my hand, the wall cannot withstand my time
Little by little breaking, things crumbling, falling apart, changing
I wonder where you are in all of this, this time bound time
Ineluctable stretch down the line, devouring everything . . .
In the late afternoon on the footbridge looking out at the river to St. Peter's
All light pierced the clouds, little by little things changing, crumbling, remade
I think you stretch beyond any human life, I wonder always where you are
Are you as near as a memory? Touching reality, hugging, smiling, always talking

—"If You Could See Me," (excerpt) by Carol Scott & Caitlin Smith Gilson

Within Every Question Is a Conversation with God

> As death, when we come to consider it closely, is the true goal of our existence, I have formed during the last few years such close relationships with this best and truest friend of mankind that death's image is not only no longer terrifying to me, but is indeed very soothing and consoling, and I thank my God for graciously granting me the opportunity . . . of learning that death is the key which unlocks the door to our true happiness. I never lie down at night without reflecting that—young as I am—I may not live to see another day. Yet not one of all my acquaintances could say that in company I am morose or disgruntled.
> —Mozart's letter to his father, 1787 (in Steptoe, *Mozart-Da Ponte Operas*)

BEFORE WE CAN TURN to the nature of heaven, we must glimpse how all human experience is in conversation with the divine. Heaven is not a far off, outdated, antiquated idea that has no place in a thoroughly modern world. Heaven is the truest and greatest yearning of every human heart. Every single question involving even an inkling of moral choice and personal dilemma is *only* compatible in a world in which God's conversation is present within each of us. The *human* questions fail even to appear in atheism.

Spiritual openness to God is united to being human. Every question from *"Is this the right choice for me?"* and *"Will I find happiness here?"* to *"Does any part of us survive death?"* are opening us up to our relationship with God. The belief in goodness deeper than opinion is grounded in daily human experience. The moment we ask questions such as *"Is this the right thing to do?"* We are connecting to a reality where some actions are better and some are worse, some choices are good and set us free, and some close us off, some decisions will have beneficial consequences which may be joyful or filled with suffering.

If goodness and badness were merely personal preferences where everyone's view is right, then the question *"Is this the right thing to do?"* wouldn't need to be raised in the first place. There would be no wrong way to be nor any right way to be! *"What am I to do?"* would likely not even be *able* to be raised if our natures were morally neutral. Goodness and truth must be more than our opinions. They must be an irreducible reality informing the universe and informing our hearts and minds. Otherwise, there would be no moral dilemmas. If there is no good and evil in existence, if there is no right way to be or wrong way to be, then there is no moral or spiritual quandary in the first place, for every answer would be as good as the next, and as meaningless as each other.

All This, and Heaven Too

"Will this make me happy?" "Will I benefit from this action?"

These questions are placing us in the mindset of divine meaning. They are putting us face to face with God, even if we do not yet realize that such questions are preambles to prayer. Why? Because a world without God is a world without meaning. Often people will say *"I do not believe in God"* or choose not to believe because *"I cannot make sense of the suffering and evils in the world,"* or *"I want to be happy, and the rules of faith are too demanding."* All these statements presuppose that meaning and goodness are something we invent. But is this true?

Let us suppose there is no God who alone can save what is lost; the alternative is that the world began by a series of material accidents. If there is no divine eternal reality, then human beings are purely material beings, as material as dirt and clay. In a world of pure materiality—if that is even possible—there can be no underlying and enduring meaning, plan, purpose to the world and to every human life. Why? In such a scenario, the world began from oblivion and is ever marching towards that oblivion. Nature dies off, the planets are not inhabitable, persons age, decline, and then die. In pure materialism, there is no guiding divine presence that informed and shaped nature, breathed meaning, spirit, and truth into all things, and designated that all things return to Him. There is instead cosmic randomness and not even a foundation for addressing the question *"Is this the right thing for me to do?"*

> All flesh is like grass, and all its glory like the flowers of the field. The grass withers and the flowers fall when the breath of the LORD blows on them; indeed, the people are grass. The grass withers and the flowers fall, but the word of our God stands forever.
> —Isaiah 40:7–8

When we ask *"Is this the right thing to do?"* the answer requires a divine order and underlying intelligence from the beginning of all time whose meaning is carried out and Who *Is* the end in which all things are directed.

- The question *"Is this the right thing to do?"* has *always* been shorthand for the following:

In terms of my unique place in this universe filled with meaning, am I freely making the right choice? Does my choice fulfill the Beauty, Goodness, and Truth, of God's order and plan, who is not indifferent to anything, but wholly invested with love in all things as Creator?

- The same question *"Is this the right thing to do?"* is a nonstarter in a universe of indifference, when it would be shorthand for:

    In terms of my random accident of existence in a universe that is also a random accident of existence, is this the right choice for me? Is my choice, compounded by countless evolutionary accidents, which have discernible patterns, such as how light refracts or gases cool, but has no overarching purpose, the right thing to do? In a world with no ultimate plan, no moral code, or any investment in my personhood, is this the right thing for me to do?

When the atheist asks the daily questions *"Is this good for me?"* or *"How do I avoid an unhappy outcome?"* he or she is undercutting that very atheism! All human questions have the annoying knack of placing one in the context of divine meaning. All questions of moral, personal, and spiritual dilemma are also *daily* questions. *"Is this the right place for me" "Is he the one to marry?" "Am I being a true friend in this situation?" "Why did she die so young?"*—place us in the reality of an invested Creator and a world responsive to that Creator.

When we say *"I will love you forever"* or cry at the bed of the loved one who has only just died and say, *"He is gone but never forgotten,"* when we raise our eyes to the starry night and ask, *"Why did this terrible event take the life of my loved one?"*—can any of these statements be meaningful in a world formed through a random collision of organic gases? Do these questions have any enduring value if spoken into an impersonal universe formed by accident and chance? All the human questions carry divine meaning, whether we acknowledge it or not. More astonishingly, there is no problem of pain and suffering without God. If the world began by an unaware, unreflective randomness against all odds, and everything is decaying, returning to dust, then the word "suffering" loses its meaning. To suffer is to experience evil. To suffer is to be deprived of some good you *should* possess. The mother *should* have the child alive, not stillborn. The father *should* have time to enjoy watching that child grow rather than lack that goodness from the start. But in a world formed by chance, which is indifferent to life, the pain experienced in returning to oblivion is the inevitable result. There is no conversation with existence. There is no supreme dialogue with matter and chance. The mother cannot claim she is deprived of the existence of the child. There is no looking to the heavens and asking: *"Why this suffering has happened to me?"* or *"Why do I feel lost?"* or *"What should I do?"* They are meaningless questions from the outset because there is no *should* in the first place. There is no God, no meaning-giver, to answer them.

Our free will and responsibility and our experience of suffering open us up to God and to whether we see God's handiwork. The questions *"What does the world or God want from me?"* and *"What do I do to realize this?"* are a deepening of the natural yearning in each of us. In this yearning we discover that:

1. Free will can set us free or make us unhappy. We are only free and happy when we act with honesty and with virtue. If we want to be free, we have an obligation to the Good. Goodness sets us free.

Our free will is only fulfilled when we direct it toward good choices. Goodness is meaningful and intelligible. Evil opposes meaning and intelligibility. Our wills become enslaved when we direct them towards evil. We have pushed them into a corner where destruction replaces creation. If our wills choose the lie, the deception, the vice, we are damaging ourselves and others. To will evil is willing one's own destruction! We cannot be happy willing evil because we are willing an end that is against our own best interests! In fact, we are closer to non-existence. When we will falsehoods, which cannot exist without defecting from the truth, we are willing ourselves into non-reality. Lies need the very truth they deny. They have a tangential existence. They do not exist on their own as substantial and actual.

Moreover, we cannot compare a state of non-existence to existence. I may be able to compare happiness to sadness because in both states I am existing, but I cannot compare a state where I am not and have no personhood with a state where I do. Our free will only grows when we realize that the discovery of our personhood is at stake. If we want to know ourselves, be free, grow, we have an obligation to the Good—for the Good sets us free.

2. We can neither escape moral obligation nor get outside God.

We cannot *not* make a choice. There is no way to bypass our responsibilities in life; we live up to them or we do not. We are asked to help our Jewish neighbor in the Holocaust. One of us refuses to make a choice, worried about the costs of each possibility. But this inactivity is *still* an action, and *still* a choice. And this inaction, which is a choice, participates in the moral fabric of the universe. Human beings must make choices. Not making a choice is making a choice. Making the choice for or against God, daily, cannot actually be avoided. There is no way to avoid God *even* as we deny Him.

3. A world without God is a world without meaning: questions reveal the divine reality.

All along we have been asking "why" questions: *Why* is there love? *Why* is there suffering? *Why* is it that without God we would not have the capacity to raise such questions in the first place? *What does the world want from me?* and *what do I need to do to realize this?* are conversations with the divine. Our free will cannot *not* make a choice. Every question we ask is a preliminary prayer placing us towards God and to the recognition that a material world cannot raise or address those questions. The world that passes away is not our permanent home.

Every question you have ever asked only has meaning because of God's foundation. They can only be answered meaningfully in reference to God. Every question is a signpost to our permanent home in heaven. There is only one person Who can satisfy these questions raised since the moment we began to wonder. Christ alone completes our questions. He is "the Way, the Truth and the Life." Through him we find our permanent home, the Good that we have always desired to possess forever.

> "Do not let your hearts be troubled. You believe in God; believe also in me. My Father's house has many rooms; if that were not so, would I have told you that I am going there to prepare a place for you? And if I go and prepare a place for you, I will come back and take you to be with me that you also may be where I am. You know the way to the place where I am going." Thomas said to him, "Lord, we don't know where you are going, so how can we know the way?" Jesus answered, "I am the way and the truth and the life. No one comes to the Father except through me. If you really know me, you will know my Father as well. From now on, you do know him and have seen him."
> —John 14:1–7

3

What Happens to Us When We Make Ourselves a Gift to the Person Who Now Has Died?

The Empty Bed, by Carol Scott

What Happens to Us When We Make Ourselves a Gift?

... Days without you, hours without you, time without your body
The unmarked eon, your cooing singularity
These things are the downed white pearl of you
Pearl to pearl, fingering each bead, Oh ... sweet, how sweet ...
Golden upward swing surfeited sweet tonic ringing body
Honeysuckle drunk silk slung fruit of the earth eaten lap
Lingering tectonic scent, trapped, packed, aromatic red cedar sap ...
We are what we are ... lucid liquefying laced lightning life on life
Take me to bed, you think we can survive this timebound beat of heart, the
    absent heat
Take me to bed, you think we can survive, the downed ember, the
    unfinished start
Take me to bed, you think we can survive the sucked-up starless night, the
    final light
I will crawl instead of speak, week broken week, recollected walk
Your body, my body, peak into valley and peak
*The who of us, the what of us, why is obvious, lovely love lust, you hear my
    heart*
Loving you circulates the air moves my blood
Loving you makes lullabies of my sleep, smoked mesquite
    Shined ruby on velvet black
Loving you

    —"What Can I Say about Loving You?" (excerpt) by Caitlin Smith
      Gilson & Carol Scott

> If a mother is mourning not for what she has lost but for what her dead child has lost, it is a comfort to believe that the child has not lost the end for which it was created. And it is a comfort to believe that she herself, in losing her chief or only natural happiness, has not lost a greater thing, that she may still hope to "glorify God and enjoy Him forever." A comfort to the God-aimed, eternal spirit within her. But not to her motherhood. The specifically maternal happiness must be written off. Never, in any place or time, will she have her son on her knees, or bathe him, or tell him a story, or plan for his future, or see her grandchild.
> —C. S. Lewis, *A Grief Observed*

The conceptual distance towards death that I once possessed relinquished itself. I am no longer a novice in grief. I have found myself inside two experiences of suffering. They must be laid bare to give the most truthful direction to this work. The first experience involves the recent death of my beloved niece, Daisi, our family's beautiful little girl. In the spring of 2020 she was struck and killed by a motorist. It was four days after her fifteenth birthday. The language of chance, probabilities, possibilities, *ifs* and *what ifs* populate every recollection. The "what ifs" act as if they are not dead-ends. They serve only to remind us that they are indeed cul-de-sacs of unresolved pain. Everything was timing: inopportune timing, bad timing, terrible, terrifying lamentable timing. If only a day later, a minute earlier and second later. Our dear girl wrapped up in the fatalism of chance.

Timing has a way of altering memories. Timing has a way of inhabiting past happiness. Everywhere timing is the aching chasm of the unfinished, unresolved, and unsaid. The horseback riding, beach bonfires, eccentric number of sneakers, snuggled scary movies under cover, funny voices made over pancakes at breakfast out, with timing these things become something other altogether. A universal story so intimate and unrepeatable. It is repeated in its own way by strangers united in sorrow. Months topple into the next. Days pile and eviscerate the many dark nights of the soul until they expel what remains of the living. The living must go on. The irony is not lost. Like so many others before us, we carry the many happy memories now laced with gall. Their deaths lance memories of their once-pure sweetness. The last time I saw Daisi is stained in my mind. My daughters and Daisi cycled around our little town in the bliss as close to *arcadia*. They went to an antique shop and picked up a curiously painted statue of the Madonna with red hair. She gave it to me and said, "She has

What Happens to Us When We Make Ourselves a Gift?

hair like yours!" All our joys have within them, for St. Thomas Aquinas, a natural foreshadowing of sadness.

We cannot escape evil. There are no utopias to be made. When they are attempted, it results in the devastation of faith and transcendence. Today's "canceling" mentality attempts to reduce evil to perception and to manage human sins as if they can be wiped off the face of the earth. This aggressive utopia-making is not original, it spans all political ideologies. Today's is a more conscious, more vicious searching for an alternative to divine meaning. Every effort to displace and replace the divine continues to deform our understanding of human nature. Our humanity is only realized in our permanent home, heaven. Grief, the gaping wound of original sin, cannot be healed by worldly power. It points beyond any worldly resolution. There are no earthly utopias that can resolve death. This unserviceability to manage or "fix" death must enter our conversations if we are to glimpse paradise.

1. The first experience, to be experienced till my *own* death, is the death of the child, and its crisis of love.
2. The second experience is the sharing of grief. The friend who has also experienced the yawning chasm. It permits tears and even permits moments of peace and love, but still, it does not allow a clarified bridge to the "other side."

What is occurring in us when we have made ourselves a gift to the person who now has died? In Christianity we are called to make ourselves a gift to persons, to love our neighbors as we love ourselves. This gift must be confronted in how it endures grief. What becomes of this self-gift when the one we love dies? How do we continue to give ourselves? How do we go on? All the power of grief is impotent. All its majestic and cruel urgency crumbles when confronted with even the most delicate remembrance of the lost child. All power falls at the feet of the absent child, and we are unable to wash her with our weeping.

Due to the thoughtfulness of my parish priest, I was put in touch with a mother who lost her child in a car accident. This accident took the lives of his friends, and it was days after learning his longtime childhood cancer was in remission. Our correspondence had the anonymity of letters. But this form conspires to unite us in ways surprising and gentle. Grace itself is at the forefront of all truly loving and generous action. Our correspondence are tears presented in another form. Perhaps they are the tears of Our Lady finding their way to earth and nourishing us with her sorrow. There is wisdom carved from holy weakness. Love and suffering fling open the gates of heaven. A whole lifetime passes through me when I see the photos of her child and read her words. My legs and arms become weakened with age, not the passing age, not even the historical age, but of a mysterious timeless power that seeps into these ages to unite our sufferings to the crucifixion. My limbs weaken to the point of no return, and yet in her compassion are rebuilt to walk anew. I sense a heaven where our families will share joy because we have shared that region of suffering. Our hearts break so purely and finely that there is no way to pick up the pieces, only to move on forever changed. But we found sources of consolation we did not know we had.

Through her letters I realize that there is a *release* that happens in the heart stricken with grief. It is a release patterned after the stigmata. The spear at Christ's side makes its way up to our heart muscles rendering them unable to pump as they did before. This release keeps recurring because there is no other alternative but to breathe again, to be distracted with *this* or *that*. And yet in the shade of such repeated release, we respond with anger and resentment for providing such interludes of peace! The pain is a kind of comfort as our lost loved one is somehow closer to us in our agony. Then, the pendulum swings. There is a resulting sadness, a different form of anger. Our weighted hearts feel sorrow and guilt for squandering that peace, for darkening the appreciation of it, for peace is a gift. Our hearts are speared by the loss of the loved one who was the recipient of our self-gift. We are broken and stretched on the rack, seeking to give love that seemingly cannot be enjoyed or returned. The interior heartache is that we are forced to release: their deaths and our living mean these releases are the inevitable pattern for the rest of our lives.

The wound of death is a perpetually re-inflicting wound. To believe it will get better is an unfair burden to put on oneself. Much of this involves clarifying the word "better." In the strict sense of things, it cannot get better, as if returned to what life was before the curtain fell. The heart is finely ground into powder. The dust has been scattered into every memory. It is not right or just that we should outlive the holy innocents. The climate of life is more violent, and the shifting seasons jagged and unfriendly. We open our eyes to an ugly world, one off kilter, and it reminds us of all the beauty that once inhabited our lives.

In the death of the loved one we *have* lost heaven. More specifically, we have lost a foretaste of the heaven Christ gave the earth when He was born of the Virgin Mary. Heaven has visited the earth. Each gift of person is a participation in the heaven Christ gave us when He was born. The death of the beloved feels like the empty tabernacle on Good Friday.

> The Incarnation is the mystery of a God who travelled the entire road toward us, and who was not only one of us during His mortal life but has remained with us, and that is not all: He dwells within us. This being so, how could we aspire to find Him elsewhere if we possess Him here on Earth? I recall the Canticle of my First Communion: "Heaven has visited the Earth." . . . Yes, and it has done more than visit the Earth, it has merged in it without annihilating itself, so that to die will be not only for us to leave the Earth but also to leave the Heaven we have possessed in the flesh even in the humiliation of sin and its tears.
> —François Mauriac, *The Inner Presence*

Part of grief's awful stubbornness is because our faith is too weak to envision heaven. Our faith is too weak to sustain genuine hope in the afterlife. We think, believe, feel, viscerally experience that we have lost it all in the death of the loved one. Part of this grief does come from an infirmed understanding of heaven as the "better place." But we also grieve with such awful humbling truth because we *have* been torn from the union that gives us a foretaste of heaven. We are the body of the church and Christ is its head. Through the Christ, the body has possessed in the flesh heaven. Still we must accept our hearts calibrated to the mystery, to the promise, and to the great hope God has given us:

> As it is written, what no eye has seen, what no ear has heard, and what no human mind has conceived the things God has prepared for those who love him—these are the things God has revealed to us by his Spirit. The Spirit searches all things, even the deep things of God.
> —1 Corinthians 2:9–10

4

Heaven Misplaced

RECOVERED THROUGH CHRIST

Contemplation, by Carol Scott

You have taken my child and I wept
Were they not enough? Those tears fed the blackthorns each Spring
They flourished just as you asked, a brutal sacrifice, Angelus lighter than air

I dreamt my children's faces in profile the morning after the fall
Quiescent rings of icing and blue frosted boat, a shoreline of shorn shells cutting our soles
The bells of Guadalupe miles beyond sight, our lives dying in us bleeding underfoot
River of the wolf, floating side by side under untouched sun

I should have grown old when you thieved my child, the weight of you in last temptation
You snatched my hands, my lips, my time, lungs sponged with the matter of your blood

I should have gone cold when you stole my child, thief in the night
Broken idea denier of earth and sky, confused shards plunged in wine

Remove this taste of the gall, God of night, God of the inner law, my lips withdraw
But you keep stealing the gentler things of my seeking
How can I love if you thieve all my sweetness?

I am your emptied verse and vessel, a rehearsal without a play
Lion without a lamb, lines without verb, grains of shoal
Wasteland of your long-call echo

You have taken my child
The blanket flower, buttercup, and lupine
The common poppy and baby blue eye
You cannot find my soul, the home of my sleep is made of coal
But long ago it was once my own
And still you stand beside the bed ready to roll away my love, my Stone of Heaven

   —"You Have Taken My Child," by Caitlin Smith Gilson

All This, and Heaven Too

For years I had the uneasy sense that the way we viewed heaven short-circuited our faith. Our personal exercise of faith leads us to this short-sighted view. Thoughts of heaven cause a subterranean terror preventing any real and prolonged contemplation. My own thoughts participated in this reduction. I had a faith short-circuited by a notion of paradise that vacillated among a comic book understanding, a vacant phrasebook expressionism, and a half-terrified desire for something truer than I would ever dare to envision.

Death obliterates conceptual distinctions and makes demands. Death follows behind with its own universal yet somehow unpredictable rules of grief and engagement. These rules are never defined by one firmly grasped earthly or finite moment, even if the event that prompts suffering is always earthly and finite. The rules of death evoke an unrepeatable experience that communicates through stasis and movement. Wherever you are, death is at the opposite end of the pendulum. Should grief enter the stillness inhabiting recollection and memory, death reminds us of movement—the sun rises, the tides change, life goes on. If you embark again on these motions of life, death reaffirms such a stasis that returns us to the coalface. We experience the impossible need for what is lost to be found and to be loved as it was, once again. Nothing is as it seems, and nothing is recovered. In the grief that separates the living from the dead, the living are compelled to a realm where worlds should never collide and inhabit the same person. But death does just that: it cultivates a new avenue of experience. It is never quite so simple to say that this *is*, this finally *is*, the road home. In every case we must pose this dilemma: either grief and suffering have no value or every value for the person. This is a particularly important decision since we live in a world that has made suffering the enemy of life, to be abolished by abortion, euthanasia, physician-assisted suicide, and the list goes on.

The loss of a real and heartfelt belief in God—and by "real," I mean an experience that is ethereal though down-to-earth, sentimental but never trite—comes from an earlier, more foundational *loss*. This is the directed desire for heaven, the personal longing for the resurrection. Have we lost what it means to *desire* the afterlife? The nature of heaven itself may play a part: mystery left unnurtured degrades into something "out-there" and unknown. It degrades further into a vague wish for immortality and finally into the blank and empty words of consolation. Or even worse, the almost comic book reduction of heaven to an earthly socialist paradise, a place where all pleasures are indiscriminately fulfilled. In this case, something too easily attainable on earth and closer to hell.

The "better place," a phrase that means well, often means nothing at all. Or worse, the "better place" becomes the very foil when approaching the mystery of grief and spiritually fruitful conversion through it. The sense of heaven may itself be further obscured. The afterlife is only thought of from within the fear of death and serves to distance us further from the homelessness that occurs in the living after the loved one fades from view. Somehow, we simultaneously remember and neglect the words of the Epistle to the Hebrews:

> For this world is not our permanent home; we are looking forward
> to a home yet to come.
> —Hebrews 13:14

The neglect of heaven is a different type of forgetting than the briefly misplaced book, only to be rediscovered in the armchair, just as intact as it was before. Heaven, which is our home, is not as easily rediscovered, nor are we as easily recovered, when death becomes yet another social inconvenience. We must be mindful of the important balance between the hidden and revealed reflections of the divine realm. Our concern is primarily that the veiled should not be confused with thoughtlessness. What happens when the yearning for heaven is repeatedly cut down during a life? When it is perilously cut closer to its roots, one day nothing, no transcendent longing, will grow again. And such a person would be so painfully far from God and from the childlike and profound wisdom of the kingdom of heaven. This work seeks to express the interior form of evangelization, the region that unites lovers bonded in the clarity of truth and the humility of mercy. Saint John Henry Newman called this region the *"cor ad cor loquitur,"* heart speaks *unto* heart. Here we are mindful that God gives us moral agency, with all the risks and rewards involved. Through this free will, and in the union of God's grace, the pearl of great price discovered. We are called *by* God *unto* God in every moment of our lives. We are free not only to ignore that call to Beauty but to put the earthly effects of that divine call out of their proper place. We can obscure the road back to our permanent home, heaven. Even the well-meaning language of the "better place," is an example of how those effects have been exiled from their proper place. This phrase creates a visibly inescapable netting across all features of human life. It entraps persons, taking even longer to recognize something is amiss, lengthening an already perilous journey to God.

We are tasked with the responsibility of heeding the divine call. God is our source of everlasting happiness. He alone promises our permanent home. This heeding evokes a twofold reality:

1. We have a moral and spiritual obligation to elevate the meaning of heaven from a homeless place outside of heart and mind.
2. We must accept the gift given through Christ to rediscover the genuine power of heaven. Through this gift we know ourselves most truly, and perhaps even for the first time.

Who we are is tied up in our permanent home. If we lose a sense of heaven and impart a dead-end version on earth, we are no longer travelers along the way but stranded without a compass or a map either to heaven or to ourselves. We recognize that any illumination of heaven must invoke a certain restraint, and seek that edifying humility to encounter the good mystery that shapes our very being.

The central defining figure, sometimes a figure of release and at other times a foil, is death. Any meditation on paradise that seeks to renegotiate the expression "a better place," must face this most elusive yet ever-present specter. Grief, loss, descent, conversion, mercy *as* judgment, judgment *as* mercy, enshrine death as if to be a halo. Death is a collision of worlds, it must make its presence known within this work and we must hold fast, seeking not to look away, but in and through death discover the path towards our true home. This collision of worlds is most supremely manifested in the figure of Christ. Jesus Christ will be our guide in navigating this interweaving of the impossible: the living and the dead, the painful and the joyous, loss and gain.

Christ gives us the keys to approach heaven:

- Christ's descent realizes the alienating possibility of hell. Hell is the type of death that *has* a sting.
- Christ's incarnation realizes and completes the fulfillment of heaven itself. Christ uniquely reflecting the union of human and divine natures.
- Through Christ we discover the mystery of grief as tragic and transcendent reality. Through Christ, we now see death as both loss and gain, there is *real* reason to weep and *real* reason to rejoice.

5

There Are Layers upon Layers of Grief

Dance Ballerina Dance, by Carol Scott

All This, and Heaven Too

I could have perished in my sorrow the day you died
Collapsed body, undernourished, broken at the window pane
Blood of my blood, I bleed for you, weep for you
Offer my stripped down ripped out joints for you
If only I could seep into deep earth where you are, dust of my dust
I think we lay in the center of stones, sleeping without dreaming, deep into cold
Everything in my crushed wailing organ cannot be touched
Too cold and too hot, too near and too far, ephemeral and weighted anchor
I cannot begin to breathe
Snowfall cannot survive the sun, melted water, feeding the soil
Depleted devastated sucked down soul drained into weeds
I could have withered in my sadness, returned to the earth
I would, if deals could be made, if life worked in that kind of trade
No one should outlive the little ones, the holiest of human beings
The child made of substance and dream, she can run along the sunlit hills for hours
Leaping and free
Corruptive life, a thief in the night, completing the Fall
Gall on my lips that day of all days
Tonight I lay with you in the center of stone, sleeping without dreaming, deep into cold
Love comes upon me, it has come upon my soul, all its colors, all its canvased light
All mercy and life, all exotic blues adorning me, un-perishing, lived again

—"I Could Have Perished in My Sorrow," by Caitlin Smith Gilson

There Are Layers upon Layers of Grief

> You have made my days a few handbreadths, and my lifetime is as nothing in your sight. Surely everyone stands as a mere breath. Surely everyone goes about like a shadow. Surely for nothing they are in turmoil; they heap up, and do not know who will gather!
> —Psalm 39:5–6

Grief is a strange predicament. Death is the one experience we cannot communicate. Yet death is the crucial experience of our lives. We are desperate to communicate its reality. A paradox created by tensions within nature. Death has a degree of naturalness, we all die. Yet it is an unnatural state to die, due to original sin. We experience this profound unnaturalness in all human reaction. We learn that an old mutual, long-out-of-touch friend who was believed to have few prospects is a highly successful lawyer, even an astronaut, we are surprised, interested to learn more, shocked even, but never the dumbfounded repetitious shock of learning of her death. Why is that? Why is the friend becoming an astronaut less shocking than learning of her death? The odds of her becoming an astronaut or a lawyer are astronomically small, unlike the odds of her dying. Death is a given. It is the sure beat, it will always win at cards. Within the strict confines of logic, an announcement of death should not promote unnerving shock. But death always has a speechlessness about it. When faced with the one inevitability of human life, we find the implicit recognition of our own sense of immortality! But death does not give us that recognition with any ease, it takes away what it gives, and then gives again what it takes away. Death *as death* appears to contradict our immortality, while at the same time confirming it. And we must live out that contradiction. Or is it a paradox? A contradiction ends in despair and in the nothingness of a dead end. A paradox, on the other hand, places us squarely within the incarnation and the events of the passion and hope for the resurrection. The contemplation of death is not in opposition to eternal life but its handmaiden. The longing for heaven is always present in the shock of death. We are unable to process death due to its intrinsic unnaturalness. Death is a state that does not reflect the grace God intended for us before the fall. Still, we must attempt to process it because we *do* die, and we are not so wounded by original sin that we cannot understand our fallen natures. To complicate and alleviate this reality, our deaths, now experienced through Christ's death and resurrection, become a supernatural good! Death is a journeying process contributing to our redemption. Every human life must experience the twofold character of death: as unable to be processed, as the unnatural and the unretrieved; and now a good to be dwelt upon since it unlocks the gates to heaven.

> I think there is no suffering greater than what is caused by the doubts of those who want to believe. I know what torment this is, but I can only see it, in myself anyway, as the process by which faith is deepened. A faith that just accepts is a child's faith and all right for children, but eventually you have to grow religiously as every other way, though some never do. What people don't realize is how much religion costs. They think faith is a big electric blanket, when of course it is the cross. It is much harder to believe than not to believe. If you feel you can't believe, you must at least do this: keep an open mind. Keep it open toward faith, keep wanting it, keep asking for it, and leave the rest to God.
> —Flannery O'Connor, *The Habit of Being*

Catholic teaching is a paradox undergirded by conflicting layers of nature. Even when we look at the many things that bring us joy (the joys as signatory of heaven)—laughter, intimacy, childhood—we find that these things are dependent upon a human nature built in layers of conflicting fabric.

Each of us is:

A. a yearning remembrance for a pre-fall state we cannot quite recall, let alone recover. We glimpse it in childlike innocence and yet long for this strange, unknown, un-grasped state of joy, which no pleasure can summon or reach. We long for this Edenic state with a stubborn and persistent wantonness. It will become the terrible hubris within all human goals and motivations, the resignation to meaningless labor, or the holy surrender necessary for faith. It is our choice.

B. in a fallen state that struggles to make good out of evil. The things we cherish have their goodness spread—indeed, woefully diluted—among natures and conditions that must be transformed to a state of perfection. To our fearful hearts and minds they may not survive such a vast transformation.

C. a participant in the flesh and blood of Christ within the twofold reality of resurrection as hope-filled promise and certitude as trust. The Christian is both certain and in total longing. We are in the presence of Christ who has already run to us and running towards Him all the same.

There Are Layers upon Layers of Grief

And the paradox of it all is that for us to long genuinely and fiercely for these transformations, we must recover how they are not lessened presences. At the same time, we must let go of every earthly love up until the moment of death. The recovery of paradise in our hearts is a strange and potentially unforgiving affair. It is also the most meaningful act of our lives. Through it we understand the meaning behind the first commandment:

> Love the Lord your God with all your heart, and with all your soul, and with all your mind.
> —Matthew 22:37

We must simultaneously experience a letting-go, a holy forgetfulness that reshapes all things, while hoping for reunion with *our* loves, not in a vague form of all-ness but in a dramatic uniqueness particular to each human person. How is that possible? And how is it to be lived out? Both unobtainable and necessary, we must find ourselves inhabiting an impossible yet essential harmony. We must be transported to the best of what life is in all its beauty, exotic and familial, but from within the very pulse of a sense of relinquishing everything that we are. We must understand with joy that to relinquish, and to be relinquished, is bliss itself while that very bliss is perfumed with the transcendent incarnation of all of earth's beautiful things.

The predicament of the Christian: we should never suppose that what death adds to the table is simply removed. This is not how salvation works. Heaven as eternal life may also be eternal dying; a fulfilled joyful surrender. These conflicting layers—the unnaturalness of death and the supernatural good of death through Christ—do not destroy each other but appear, impossibly so, to live in a conversation that realizes our highest happiness. We experience the agony of grief, and it does not cancel or mute the experience of the joy of passive purification intrinsic in dying. Both experiences are fully present and define the meaning of our transcending human flesh. We do not simply "get better" from the grief over the loss of the child—the natural order has and will always be on this earth inverted, and everything on earth serves to remind us of what is missing.

> Grief fills the room up of my absent child,
> Lies in his bed, walks up and down with me,
> Puts on his pretty looks, repeats his words,
> Remembers me of all his gracious parts,
> Stuffs out his vacant garments with his form;
> Then, have I reason to be fond of grief?
> —Shakespeare, *King John*

The cross has lifted us out of that unnaturalness of death, but this transcendence is not magic; it does not wipe away the reality of the world as irredeemable without Christ's grace and mercy. This is the risk of grief when the child is beyond earthly reach. The healing that comes from faith always springs from the recognition that death is and will always be a gaping wound. We can say without contradiction that the holy innocents are now home. With God they miss nothing and gain everything. We must also acknowledge the sheer immeasurable loss and alienation housed in death, and at its apex in Christ, when He asks if the cup can be passed. Otherwise, what do we make of the millions of aborted babies, of the lives lost before they began? Heaven is home, but earth is always the *way* home.

This is how we live out the paradox of death as simultaneously a natural experience and a profoundly unnatural state. All of us experience a degree of this paradox when we live and die, and none is immune to it. But death of the great love places us within that gaping wound that is ever un-healing and simultaneously healed, but only through Christ. We often forget that Christ overcame death through His death. He had to die to overcome it, He had to die to be resurrected. That is why grief is a participation in crucifixion, and it is this saddest of all states that alone brings us into the meaning of heaven, not merely as "better place" but in all its hard-won majesty. Each of us is already inside the twofold nature of death as simultaneously both the experience of terrifying loss and the confirmation of our immortality. Neither experience expels the other. And this odd potent experience will be with us for the rest of our lives. It is the death sentence releasing us from death! It is loss *as loss*, while being gain! Neither does the loss outwit the gain, nor does the gain undercut the loss on this side of eternity. Christ's love gifts us with the way through His wound, and the way *is* the wound, for Christ has risen with His scars. We receive salvation hiding in His wounds. This is the rosary of tears that begins in the memory of innocence and in the blood shared by all.

> For the word of God is alive and active. Sharper than any double-edged sword, it penetrates even to dividing soul and spirit, joints and marrow; it judges the thoughts and attitudes of the heart.
> —Hebrews 4:12

We never overcome that tragic sense on this side of eternity. We carry both of those experiences, recognizing that neither experience cancels out the other. This is the first insight into recovering paradise from merely the unexamined festival. Only in a life where the terror of the loss of our loved ones is felt as irremediable *and* experienced through the gift of the cross as immeasurable gain and loving, delightful joy, can we approach what is won for us in our permanent home. That is our cross, which we must bear. Neither experience erases the other, which means both experiences are felt in their dramatic power and exigency. Only in paradise, through Christ's grace, is the experience of loss finally canceled out. Heaven is not a bloodless utopia but the font of healing water in which our whole beings emerge, the estuary of release that finally *does* release. Paradise is dance with laughing and singing and praise, so magnificent that tears of sheer nectar spring forth.

> My son, eat honey, for it is good, and the drippings of the honeycomb are sweet to your taste. Know that wisdom is such to your soul; if you find it, there will be a future, and your hope will not be cut off.
> —Proverbs 24:13–14

6

The Hunt for Heaven

The Tale Underneath All Tales

Flying to Infinity and Beyond, by Carol Scott

... If nothing of me remained, I would still love the salt of you
The anything, the everything that survived the death of minds
When I burn up, disintegrate, passing through atmosphere, caressing you
Hurtling down, I will hear your voice, the sound of water, passing through my riverbed
Universe of you, completing you, amplifies sound, condenses silence
Pleasures the abyss, refines thought, reified life-bringer, fire-giver
Immersed in water, moments before ice and winter
You are inside and outside pulling me, bright and dark ...
All my sun and moons multiplying, dividing into singular image
Your face at the door, your head on my breast, the one stilled glimpse
Moving through me, universe of you ... I feel your pull
Halving, merging, gutting, subduing, loving
I feel your pull bring me down on these knees
Across the leagues of spirit and soul
Wave breaker, our universe of yours and mine ...
Splitting apart
Moaning till the rotation comes around, ego eclipsed into a ring of fire
Ecstasy dancing, happy backstroking, floating
Resting in our love

—"We are Swimming between Universes,"
(excerpt) by Carol Scott & Caitlin Smith Gilson

All This, and Heaven Too

Heaven is the summit and joy of human existence and, at the same time, neglected. We understand it to be the estuary of the Good in which we shall have no other desire than to remain there eternally. Unseen at present, it is, in fact, the only reality truly experienced *as is*. Paradise is the precious crown and treasure; and that either we suffer here in this world through our ardent yearning for God or suffer in the next through our obstinate denial of Him. Yet still, in all of this, heaven escapes us. I mean that the very texture, the filling, the tender substance of the place, state, or realm eludes capture with a pervasive persistence. Because we are unable to focus our lens to get a substantial glance, we are historically tempted to focus our belief on those so-called "more important" things. Yes, those things are important to the faith, but only within the context of salvation, and salvation is homecoming, and homecoming is heaven. All roads lead to heaven, from the beginning to the end. And it is the little things, the specifics, the minutiae that have *always* characterized a human life embodied by time, memory, hope, dream, flesh, and blood. Thus, the longer way of embodied human life cannot be bypassed in the architecture of heaven because heaven is realized in Christ.

In unity with Christ, our flesh and blood are given a permanence and dignity beyond a brief and fleeting moment in time. Our bodies are shot through with eternity. The radicality of Christ's gift to us is stunning. Christ is God and flesh, heaven itself is incarnated too, uniting the spirit and flesh, the eternal and time, the divine and human. Wounded as it may be, our own flesh still gives us a glimpse into heaven. We are neither angels nor beasts; instead, we stand on the horizon between time and eternity. What can we grasp of heaven that properly reflects the created nature God gave us and that Christ realized in the incarnation? Perhaps this state of blindness, this unclarified stance, is precisely the point. We are to be in the dark, we are not ready, nor worthy, and ever in need of grace. But at the same time, if we leave that sightlessness unnurtured, unattended, does heaven, the only place we will ever truly see *as is*, devolve into empty ideas? And then what could we ever see? Christ's incarnation is innumerably wondrous. When Christ realizes heaven for human beings, He does so by merging—and without annihilation—the presence of heaven on earth and even, and more secretly, the presence of earth in heaven. In heaven resides the taste, the hunger for the earthy, the carnal, the dust and the clay, transfixed and transposed.

> *Our Father who art in Heaven,* he knew very well what he was doing that day, my son who loved them so.
> Who lived among them, who was like one of them.
> Who went as they did, who spoke as they did, who lived as they did.
> Who suffered.
> Who suffered as they did, who died as they did.
> And who loved them so, having known them.
> Who brought back to Heaven a certain taste for man, a certain taste for the Earth.
> My son who loved them so, who loves them eternally in Heaven.
> He knew very well what he was doing that day, my son who loved them so.
> —Charles Péguy, "I Am Their Father"

This twofold union of heaven's foretaste on earth and earth's carnality permeating heaven impresses upon us an anti-fantasist human nature stretching towards heaven. The desire for heaven is not a peripheral yearning compared to life's goals. It is not a wish-fulfilling sentiment soon left at the wayside from childhood to maturity. Instead, heaven is what finally unveils and completes our human nature. The Father is *only* Father in relation to the Son, and the Son is *only* Son in relation to the Father. The Father, like the Son, has given Himself *need*. That need is for their home to be our home. God is only home because we—in our flesh and blood realized in Christ—audaciously fulfill heaven supported by God's sheer eternal presence. This is the true "happily ever after."

> Still, let us both take heart of hope and of faith. The link between father and son is not only of the perishable flesh: it must have something of *aeternitas* about it. There is a place called "Heaven" where the good here unfinished is completed; and where the stories unwritten, and the hopes unfulfilled, are continued. We may laugh together yet.
> —J. R. R. Tolkien's letter to his son, Michael, during WWII

Christ has given to human beings far more than we deserve. "We are not worthy for You to enter under our roof, but only say the word." The Word has been incarnated and the roof is formed in this unity of God's spiritual eternity and human embodiment. What Christ has given us is Himself, a forming power within the very architecture of paradise!

The wellspring of theological and philosophical discussion on the nature of the human person in relation to God have not been thoroughly applied to heaven. We need to dwell on the concrete questions each human person raises when confronted with death and the possibility of the afterlife. St. Paul understood heaven to be our true home. What happens to our human nature when heaven is set aside? This causes a loss in genuine belief in God, and in the formation of a Christian community. Tertullian's *I believe because it is astonishing, unbelievable, too beautiful, and good*, loses all its invitational power and becomes what it opposes: a defense that belief itself is unworthy of belief! How can we search for heaven if it is not central to questions of human nature? When undreamt by our flesh and blood, we deny our humble but central role in forming the architecture of heaven. For too long we have attempted to define human nature exclusively through the things of earth. This is the present crisis of the secular world. Materialism, relativism, and subjectivism reign supreme. How can heaven be anything other than an afterthought if materiality constitutes the meaning of humanity? The nature of the human person becomes an inquiry that cannot even begin to be asked! We are seeking to recover the natural capacity to seek out heaven. But we are faced with a fallen world where that desire has been dramatically deformed by the denial of death, the hoarding of pleasures, until there is nothing more than oblivion in place of consciousness.

When the afterlife is no longer imagined, desired, envisioned as a dramatic commingling of friendship, love, and surrender, its architecture recedes to the depository of thoughtlessness. Heaven is reduced to the unthought festival that secretly begins the turn away from God more than any atheism. All atheisms begin in a misunderstood human nature. The greatest error originates in the loss of heaven. Our human nature is realized only in our permanent home. While the human soul does have a mode of knowledge separate from the body, where we survive after death, we are not angels. We must not misconceive heaven as if we were disembodied angels. This view would relinquish the true joy, the happiness and community reflecting our embodiment endowed by our Creator. Our souls were not produced before our bodies. Such a creation would undermine the very nature of the soul and body relationship. The human soul is *for* the benefit of the body and the human body *for* the benefit of the soul. Any sense of heaven that undercuts this created unity is far more cartoon than Catholic and more unworthy of belief.

Heaven is not merely a better dressed earth. We must also see what *is to be seen* in this world of penultimate joys is an inkling of the paradisal home to come. We must recover the unbroken thread within our flesh and blood that connects us to the one truly Good Reality. Heaven is the fairytale to end all fairytales. It may be too good for us, but not too good to be true. We must recover this thread from the thoughtless notion of a "better place." The better place hasn't enough substance to be the estuary where all desires flow in ecstasy and surrender. Christ is the great reality, the backbone of existence. Our Savior is the greatest story ever told precisely because He accomplishes the innermost yearning of the fairytale. Our thread is trust, the painful and graceful trust that rises as fragrance within us. Happy are we who trust in Christ. All true joy rests on His story, which fulfills all stories. Christ alone achieves what all fairy tales anticipate and seek: the *happily ever after*. Our happily ever after is completed in His "*It is finished*," wherein suffering as totalizing abandonment becomes the place for union, joy, peace, and play:

> I saw, while looking at the same cross, that His blessed expression changed. The changing of His blessed expression changed mine. . . . Then our Lord made me think happily, "Where is there not one jot of your pain or your sorrow?" And I was very happy. I understood that we are now, as our Lord intends it, dying with Him on His cross in our pain and our passion; and if we willingly remain on the same cross with His help and His grace until the final moment, the countenance He turns on us will suddenly change, and we shall be with Him in Heaven . . . and everything will be turned to joy.
> —St. Julian of Norwich, *Revelations of Divine Love*

When Christ realizes heaven through His incarnation, He gives us the fertile ground to long for our home. In the church we are gifted with the true celebration—solemnity and joy, death and life—not the superficial celebrations that avoid death at all costs. The worldly festivity is the unthought acceptance of the soul as accidentally united to the body or the soul as nothing more than the body. These serious misunderstandings vacate the body ennobled by Christ. Our bodies are more than transitoriness and are the overflowing presence of the divine. Our bodies in Christ are rivers as bright as crystal, and trees yielding fruit, where there is no longer any night because the face of God will be brighter and warmer than the light of lamp or sun.

The laborer may finally put down his axe and shovel. He may enter the field of play, where walking turns into leaping and dancing, and words melt into singing and praise. The fairytale imagines perfection, but must leave it undefined, framed by the closing lines "happily ever after." The story of

Christ's gift is the happily ever after because He breaks the chains of death. Christ fulfills all true stories by inviting us to share in His glorified body. We should pant like the deer for heaven. Christ's gift is no mere narrative of wishes and ideals. When we place Christ within the "better place" that cannot capture or enrapture a heart, we lose ourselves in the process. We have lost Christ as the very story of life itself. Our faith is for the childlike, not the childish. Heaven is for the warrior, not the coward. And this is so often misunderstood. We are called to recover the dramatic desire to enter the beauty of the truest story. Through it, the love, hope, and redemption of transfigured souls is accomplished. What happens to a culture, particularly a religious culture, when its underlying tale of all tales is diminished? It is a critical indicator that something is amiss. Why is it that today so few theologians are saints? The practice of theology and the quest for sanctity have not only undergone a trial separation, seen other people, explored life apart, but even accepted their divorce with the pride of a secularist badge of honor.

The deepest tale of all tales permeates the soil of existence and directs culture to flower. The transcendent expressions of faith and sanctity deepen every facet of life. Western Civilization is most deeply an expression of Christ's incarnation, and we can see today why the Catholic Church is so much under attack, both from within and without. If contemporary Western culture is to change, overcome, and "cancel" Christianity, it must subvert Judeo-Christian values. It first intimidates the faith into a private-only existence, then through a hostile neglect causes these values to wither away. The roots of faith die without the sunlight of natural public practice. When virtues are exercised only privately, they will inevitably become the basis for a deceitful civilizational decline, one that dresses up mob-mentality as wisdom and prudence. Christ's heaven is the greatest *tale* of all tales because it is transcendent Truth. Christ enables all other myths, fables, hopes, and dreams to spring up and yearn for sunlight like the winter's tulip. Chesterton reminds us of these long untended roots:

> About all these myths my own position is utterly and even sadly simple. I say you cannot really understand any myths till you have found that one of them is not a myth. Turnip ghosts mean nothing if there are no real ghosts. Forged bank-notes mean nothing if there are no real bank-notes. Heathen gods mean nothing, and must always mean nothing, to those of us that deny the Christian God. When once a god is admitted, even a false god, the Cosmos begins to know its place: which is the second place. When once it

is the real God the Cosmos falls down before Him, offering flowers in spring as flames in winter. "My love is like a red, red rose" does not mean that the poet is praising roses under the allegory of a young lady. "My love is an arbutus" does not mean that the author was a botanist so pleased with a particular arbutus tree that he said he loved it. "Who art the moon and regent of my sky" does not mean that Juliet invented Romeo to account for the roundness of the moon. "Christ is the Sun of Easter" does not mean that the worshipper is praising the sun under the emblem of Christ. Goddess or god can clothe themselves with the spring or summer; but the body is more than raiment. Religion takes almost disdainfully the dress of Nature; and indeed Christianity has done as well with the snows of Christmas as with the snow-drops of spring. And when I look across the sun-struck fields, I know in my inmost bones that my joy is not solely in the spring, for spring alone, being always returning, would be always sad. There is somebody or something walking there, to be crowned with flowers: and my pleasure is in some promise yet possible and in the Resurrection of the dead.
—G. K. Chesterton, *A Miscellany of Men*

The Christian faith has always been a faith practicing death. Now we are practicing the death of the faith. This conflation exists throughout our culture and has taken stronghold in academia. The faith is being hounded out of existence by a tidal wave of vicious concessions that render it meaningless, dulling its beauty and whitewashing its teachings. How then can we evangelize effectively and reinvigorate the goodness of this salvific faith? There are no easy ways and means. Each of us is lost in varying degrees because each is fallen. Many of us believe our fallenness is the new lodestar of virtue. We are nomadic because this earth, while at times a loving promise to be our home, is itself not. This necessitates that all the teachings of the faith, from the theology of the body, to the sanctity of life, to the last things, lose their magnetic power when they are not presented within their proper place: hope for heaven. How can we spread the beauty of the faith if we have not tended to its roots, to the mythic pattern of paradise fulfilled in Christ? By the deepest story, we do not mean an invented narrative, fable, or tale that ends only as a narrative, a fable. These cannot complete the human yearning for the divine. We mean the mystical wisdom so holy, inviting, and pure that it is understood only through consecrated experience. Christ's heaven is the ground from which spring all tales and all love songs. Until we recover an incarnated vision of paradise, we may indeed have theologians, doctors, maids, accountants, lawyers, plumbers, farmers, but we will not have saints. We will not have faith that drips like sap from the maple and nectar from comb. What is the good of a proclaimed "good life" if such goodness does not saturate our very being? To find this fertile soil, we must return to our roots, the heaven that Christ's flesh realizes within our own bodies and souls. Any genuine appreciation of eternal happiness that elevates us beyond nullifying utopias requires an in-depth reflection on the sense of purgatory both before and after death. Paradise cannot be a cosmetically better earthly existence, nor can it be so estranged from what embodiment denotes. What can and must we say of our home that for so long has been a strange and foreign land?

7

Do We Lack and Long in Heaven without Our Bodies?

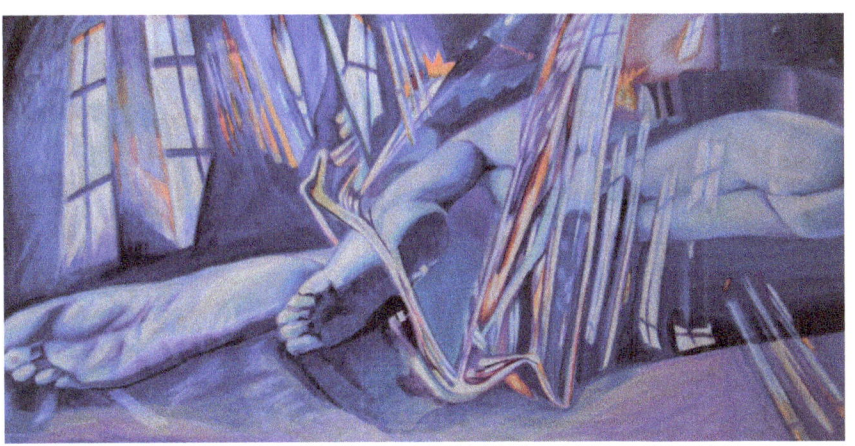

St. Teresa in Ecstasy, **by Carol Scott**

All This, and Heaven Too

God bathes on the top of your tongue
Glass candy yellow red liquefied soothsaying
Decadent salvation, bodily praying

Your hands, drawn warmed feathering
Your touch, shattering into intervals of anticipation
You part me perfectly

I could not crave your body more
Right now
Right when the sun sinks down
Purple cape of lowered light
Divination in the deep of your time
Growling incarnations chase and align
Crown the night
Long long waiting line
Landscapes after landscapes of you

Search me out, make your demands
Turn me over upside down
There are so many lands between us
I wish you were here
Voyeur of slow motion
Your ineluctable image flow
Irresistible thievery
Wreathing your sighs

I could not crave you more
When the moon is at its peak, shining black sheet
The unspoken word of your anatomy
The word of your soul
The word of your spirit
Descending on me
I wish you were here

   —"Split Apart," by Caitlin Smith Gilson

Do We Lack and Long in Heaven without Our Bodies?

At the outset, the answer must be "no." This is heaven, paradise after all. It is our union with the only Source of happiness, God. It is a perfect union without any impediment. And yet, such a state of happiness, should it be attained after death, is *without* our bodies. We are not angels, we were never meant to be without our bodies or to die. Death is a result of sin. How we learn, grow, and love has always been *through* our bodies. Our happiest memories connect us to experiences of the body: touch, taste, smell, sight, hearing. Who would trade holding your child, feeling her cheek against your face, smelling the sweetness of her little newborn head? Even Christ saves us *through* the dignity of His body. Is our happiness really achieved in a disembodied state? Wouldn't such a happiness without our bodies be more difficult than we realize? This is a strange predicament.

For St. Thomas Aquinas, the human soul is immortal and survives death, continuing to exist after the separation from the body. Yet Aquinas recognizes the troubling predicament. The soul's union with the body is essential to it. It is the very nature of a unique human soul to animate a particular human body—*your* soul for *your* body. Every human soul realizes its purpose by dwelling in the body for which it was made. The soul helps the body be what it is, as the body helps the soul fulfill its aims. My soul is uniquely *for* my body as your soul is uniquely *for* your body. The job of our souls is one that they desire. We know that a body without a soul is lifeless, dead. The soul is higher in dignity compared to the body, but it is still to the determinant of the soul to be without its body. Yes, the soul survives death, but is not its state much like a loving spouse without its helpmate, its beloved?

> Without the body, the soul is in an unnatural condition; and what is unnatural cannot go on forever. Therefore the soul, which is perpetual, is not forever apart from the body but will be united with it. The soul's immortality, therefore, seems to demand the eventual Resurrection of body.
> —St. Thomas Aquinas, *Summa Contra Gentiles*

Some of the hesitancy we face when attempting to dwell on heaven is rooted in the crisis of the separated soul. If the human soul should never separate from the body, there is understandable confusion living within us when faced with our own death. It is difficult to understand the actual state of our loved ones who have died. For good reason, it is hard for us to imagine a state where our dear child is not running in the backyard, where her face isn't beaming red with a smile that radiates joy. It is hard to imagine that same child without hands, feet, soft cheeks, eyes that shine. Perhaps it is impossible to conceive of a state where the weight of that child's head resting on our laps is no more. We often choose to avoid considering the state of heaven without our bodies. To dwell on such a state gets us uncomfortably closer to non-existence than we would like to admit. We push that fear down into the abyss where the well-intentioned "better place" resides. But grief has its own reckoning and will push us to face these uncomfortable questions. Let us remember that faith is not built on a house of cards. There is a way to understand this state of the separated soul. We need to uncover what it means to be in heaven without a body.

Here is the difficulty: the human soul is made to dwell in and define the human body. Each human body achieves its power to act, grow, and learn *through* the soul made for it. The soul directs, guides, and completes its aims *through* the body made for it. It is this union that makes each human person distinct and unrepeatable. If this is the relationship between the soul and body, how can it be claimed that we do not lack and long for our bodies in heaven? At the same time, how *can* we lack perfection, and audaciously make this claim, now wholly united with God? The state of the separated soul presents a crisis regarding the dignity of each human person.

St. Thomas Aquinas responds to an attempt to circumnavigate the problem at hand. We understand that what God intends is what *should* survive. How God created human beings reflects what should endure. Something unnatural cannot last. A lie, for example, may convince temporarily but because it opposes God's design it cannot last and has no place in heaven. The objector argues that each human soul was created beforehand, separate from the body in which it will subsequently dwell. If this were the case, then we can square the circle of heaven without our bodies. God created souls first, He intended souls to last, not bodies. But this argument does not hold for a multitude of reasons, and listed are just a few:

- This would mean that our bodies, the world, nature, all material reality are an afterthought. It would mean that we are better off without them if our only nature is to be a soul only.
- It would mean that the human soul cannot do its job very well if it was created without reference to the body and now dwells in a body and as an afterthought.
- It would call into question God's perfection and goodness for making such an anachronistic and unjust creation. Why would God make the

human person as a stuffing together of two elements, soul and body, which are not designed for each other?

The soul outlasts the body due only to sin. The *proper* unity of each human soul and body requires that each was formed together at the same time, reflecting their essential relationship. This forming of soul and body together reflects the dignity of each human person. It also reflects the intended desire of God that we should know and love Him as persons, body and soul. It is a disproportionate reality that the soul outlasts the body. This is due to the defect of the body through original sin causing death. We cannot square the circle and argue that souls were made before and separately from their bodies. Are we to concede then that the end in heaven, as a separated soul, is *not* proportionate to the beginning? And if we do accept this reality, are we calling heaven a disproportionate, even a shockingly unnatural, state? The soul is united to a body, the soul was not created before the body, but *with* it. Can we really claim that the state of the disembodied soul, no matter how good it is in heaven, is in its perfection?

We enter yet another predicament. All our knowledge—from everyday experiences, such as understanding the differences between cups and glasses, to transcendent experiences, such as love and goodness—begin in sensory human experience. Human experience *always* involves our bodies and the senses that bring information to our souls. We can feel the difference between the cup and the glass, we can hear the difference as they are tapped with a spoon to make a toast. Our senses react to different experiences. Our souls help decipher that information as love or honesty, a virtuous act or one filled with vice. Our senses bring data to the intellect. The intellect realizes these experiences as fear, joy, pleasure, comfort, and so on. If the human soul is made to dwell in its human body and the body is made for its soul, can we quite simply say that sensory experience can be bypassed in the process of knowledge? Remember: heaven is a state of separated souls. Therefore, how do we *know* in heaven? There is no body present to experience the squeeze of the embrace, the fragrance of the valley. In heaven, there are no eyes, ears, touch, taste, and smell to supply the soul not only with its whereabouts but with the foundations for the soul to process this information as awe, beauty, and sublime reality. The angels, who were never made to have bodies, understand heaven. But they were made for such a state, their spirits were not made with bodies. To say that in heaven we understand *like angels* is a misunderstanding of the human soul, as though it is better off without the body or was never made to be *with* a body. Neither is the case.

Aquinas goes to great lengths to show that in our separated state, contrary to many objections, we do in fact have knowledge. This is necessary if Aquinas is to claim heaven as the perfect happiness for humans. But the Angelic Doctor understands the delicacy, almost impossibility, of clarifying such a position. Aquinas teaches us that it is natural for the soul to turn to the body to receive its knowledge. He also reaffirms that it is unnatural for the soul to be separated from the body and separated from *how* it derives knowledge. But we are reminded of our unique place between heaven and earth. We are like angels in that we can, unlike all other animals, knowingly reflect on divine things. Only humans and angels are in the image and likeness of God. But we are unlike angels because we experience the divine and eternal things—such as perfection, truth, goodness, beauty, existence, love, mercy—*through* temporal, material experiences. The physical, temporal holding of a hand signifies the *eternal* good of love, the physical, temporal weeping at the gravesite signifies the hope for God's *eternal* mercy. We share with animals a corporeal kinship—we learn *through* our bodies, through the world. It is quite true that the body is not united to the soul accidentally. If it were, such difficulties as to how we have knowledge in our separated state would quickly vanish. But because it is the soul's very nature, for its own good, to be united to a body, St. Thomas must illustrate how the soul can receive knowledge authentically when separated from its body. He must do so without trampling on that sacred union of body and soul that God created for each human being.

The key is our *image* and likeness to God. Within the order of creatures, human beings are the highest of all material beings. We are higher than all animals but the lowest of all spiritual beings, placed lower than angels. The sun sets and spreads brilliant color across the water. This is the horizon line, a boundary between night and day. We are on the horizon line between time and eternity, between the material world and spiritual realm. It is our nature to live on that line, to reside between two states. As the Gospels tell us, we are *in* but not *of* the world. It is a great good and beauty to take in more of God's creation than any other animal. We can see the forest from the trees. The animal may perceive the trees and have pleasure running in the woods, but we can do that and so much more. We understand that this forest is the Ardennes. We can rise above nature and connect with the immaterial and spiritual significance of the place. We can find the tree where our great grandfather lay dying and imagine him shivering, saying a prayer, seeking his mother with sorrow and fear competing with peace and exhaustion. We may say a prayer in the present moment for all those young soldiers who died in the Great Wars in those woods, deep in memory amid numberless sunsets. We are the highest of the animals because we are *simultaneously* the lowest of spiritual beings. We have the great capacity to experience divine and transcendent reality. This means we *do* have the capacity to be fulfilled in the state of the separated soul in heaven.

8

How Are Humans (for Once) Higher Than Angels?

City Park with the Girls, by Carol Scott

How Are Humans (for Once) Higher Than Angels?

Your life well lived is my happiness, your love of God will be my todays
Between sleep and sky, I will love and pray for you
I cannot count the tomorrows, that the fates allow
But your presence seems to ride time, your purpose brings me back to life
Impact, brighter, truer, felt, your realism, your compassion
Incense through night and day, I believe you can make anything
Your fantastical insights, your guarded sweetness, spirit given as gift
I love that the one who shares my heart can make anything
You soothe me in my sorrow, your love of body
All bodies in love, your ways move me, you move my mind and my heart
You have all the next moves
You move my body because my heart is permanently moved
Your beauty could make anything
It already has
You are
Ever grounded and always free
Quite simply you amaze me

   —"The One Who Shares My Heart Can Make Anything," by Caitlin Smith Gilson

All This, and Heaven Too

AQUINAS'S RESOLUTION NEVER FORSAKES the difficulty, paradox, and ever-present crisis inherent in the state of the separated soul. This is a crisis for too long sidestepped by the "better place." Dante in the *Divine Comedy* understood the predicament of souls separated from the good of their bodies. The more deeply we enter the *Inferno*, the more the damned are disconnected from goodness and any desired connection to God. These shades lose any semblance of their human shape. The shades become deflated, elongated, misshapen, much like a balloon popped, having lost its purpose. In contrast, in the *Purgatorio* we have an inkling of the desire for the resurrected state, when we hope to receive our glorified bodies. These souls, filled with the desire for unity with the divine light, push out from their spirits, as if in labor pains, an immaterial or aerial body. This image of a body is more than a shadow, it is a shape that illuminates and has a beauty to it and an inviting human form. We are reminded that there is a unique dignity to human embodiment that is never sidestepped in heaven.

In the order of creatures, from animals to humans and angels, truly it is higher and nobler to be like the angels who receive perfect knowledge by turning directly to God rather than having to deal with the exhaustive *longer way* of discovering the divine through the passage of a human life. Our lives are marked with the struggle for knowledge, fallibility, health issues, grief, and death. Again: while never having a body befits an angel, it does not befit a human soul. This would render the body accidental to the soul, which would wholly undermine the integrity of human nature and God's material creation. If there is no upside to the body, why would a good and all-knowing God create us in this way? We have the capacity to arrive at eternal truths like the angels, but unlike angels we must do so through time and embodiment, a path fraught with perpetual struggle. Why would God handicap us if there is no good to it? What would be the point of it all?

What does it mean to be in the image and likeness of God? All creation has likeness to God, for things *unknowingly* reflect the good, order, purpose, design, and plan of their Creator, Whose imprint is upon their finest detail. Only two beings have *image* and likeness: angels and humans. To possess *image*, creatures must *knowingly* understand their creation. These creatures must act on the moral and spiritual obligations and gifts that come from free will and from their capacity to love God and to be loved by God. Because angels are higher spiritual beings, deriving their knowledge directly from God's eternal presence, they are more perfectly in *image* to God than human beings. We must work to glimpse the eternal good through temporal reality. We share an inkling of the eternal power of love, but it is discovered slowly through our own earthly experiences of love—love of the child, the spouse, the friend. Each human love is individualized, and each undergoes the passage of time, the response to free will, moral obligation, good and evil. Some loves are more perfected and some less perfected in relation to the divine image of love. While our correspondence to divine love is fallible due to this *indirect* relation to God, the angel's image is direct and infallible, wholly united to God as Source. Therefore, when the angels fell, their fall is permanent and unredeemable. Angelic knowledge is without error. They *know* immeasurably more the radical truth that only God ensures happiness, existence, and goodness. Still angelic knowledge, as unthinkable as it is to us, does not prevent the exercise of their free will. They were free to defect from goodness, defect from God. The angels were free to defect even from the certitude of truth and union with God. Because their image to God is the highest, their fall is unredeemable, properly reflecting their knowledge before the fall.

Human beings while on earth have the capacity, unlike any other earthly creature, of falling into sin and falling away from God. We have this capacity because like angels we are in the image of God. But our image is discovered through fallible means such as time, embodiment, grief, and earthly loves. We enter conversation with our image and likeness to God through degrees of experience. Our sinful fall on earth is not permanent; there is always time to turn around, to ask for God's forgiveness, even on our death beds.

> Now that my ladder's gone
> I must lie down where all the ladders start
> In the foul rag and bone shop of the heart.
> —W. B. Yeats, "The Circus Animals' Desertion"

There is an advantage but also a dignity to having an image to God that is lower than the angels. We can see that our image to God affords a certain safety net. The angels being beyond time and having infallible knowledge means their sinful fall is permanent. But we are given second, third, and innumerable chances. This reflects God's grace and our natures as lived out on this horizon between time and eternity. If we focus a little more on that safety net, there is an additional positive aspect that places us *relatively* higher than even angels! We have the likeness that pertains to all created things who naturally and *unknowingly* reflect the order, plan, goodness, and beauty of their Creator. Look at, for example, the magnificent biological design of the human body that allows us to think, understand, and to feel genuine sentiment. We also have an *active* likeness to God that sets us apart from both animals and angels. This active or reflective likeness is a crucial part of human dignity. We have the capacity to reflect *knowingly* on our image to God. Through virtuous actions, we liken ourselves ever more deeply to God's image, which is infinitely and inexhaustibly Good. This is a gift most particular to human beings and gives us a dignity separate from the angels.

Reflect on the following example. We can make a copy of Van Gogh's *Sunflowers*, and over time keep perfecting our colors, textures, and perspective. But at a certain point there is nothing more to be done. Our painting has achieved proficiency and a quality that renders it as a near-perfect copy of the original. There is nothing more to gain; we have exhausted ourselves in likeness and knowledge of this *finite* object of art. The journey of discovery cannot go on forever, and at a certain point we have accomplished a perfect copy of the painting. But we are in the image and likeness of God. Our Lord created all things and is *infinite*. God is without beginning or end and is Goodness, Truth, Beauty, Happiness, and Love itself. We are in the image and likeness of such a humbling Source. God is the only source that enables us to engage in an endless and ever-growing conversation with the highest things! Unlike copying Van Gogh's *Sunflowers*, we are not copies of anything. We become more originally ourselves by entering that personal conversation the Creator has set out for each of us in the journey of our lives. Our lives can be an intensified and personal reflection on our image to God. This is our unique relationship with God. This is our likening power throughout our lifetime. We finite and temporal beings can shape ourselves in accordance with God's inexhaustible, infinite, and eternal love. This is how we are *relatively* higher than the angels. We can discover our image and likeness to God and engage in a lifetime of crafting a deeper likeness. While the image of God is far more perfect in the angel than in the human person, we have a dignity, a likening power, within the *entirety* of our bodies and souls that can raise us above the angels. Our bodies reflect and participate in this likening power. This dignity is at its supreme fulfillment in God becoming human, Christ's flesh and blood.

Think about the power of our image and likeness in hearing God's Word. We were made to hear the Word Who "was made flesh and dwelt among us full of grace and truth." Hearing is not a mere collating of random unrelated sounds; when we hear, we are obeying reality and truth, making *sense* of the sounds. We conform our beings to understand the sound, entering a greater *likeness* with the sound as meaning. Only if there is a *way* for things to be is there meaning, otherwise one has indecipherable noise. In hearing, our senses are triggered, the soul responds allowing the whole person, body and soul, to take on the likeness of the sounds as words and meanings. This is why a foreign language sounds too quick, run together, indistinct. This remains the case until the sound hides and the real pattern, action, meaning comes to the forefront. This occurs through gained understanding, a gained *likeness* to the meaning within the sounds. Just as in learning a new language, all genuine hearing intrinsically involves a turning of one's whole being to the words. This is an *obedience* to a deeper likeness with that reality of the word and its promise of truth. Only when the foreign language ceases to be heard as sound and finally is heard as meaning, do we arrive at the depth of hearing *as obedience*. In hearing, we turn our whole being to the word to take in what is offered by that word. This is most truly the case when Christ is the Word. Our likeness to God grows immeasurably when we respond with our whole beings to the Word, becoming like the Word.

> Do not let your hearts be troubled. You believe in God; believe also in me. My Father's house has many rooms; if that were not so, would I have told you that I am going there to prepare a place for you? And if I go and prepare a place for you, I will come back and take you to be with me that you also may be where I am. You know the way to the place where I am going.... Anyone who loves me will obey my teaching. My Father will love them, and we will come to them and make our home with them. Anyone who does not love me will not obey my teaching. These words you hear are not my own; they belong to the Father who sent me.
> —John 14:1–4, 23–24

In hearing, we can see the power of our active likeness to God that is higher than the angels. The Word may only be sounds at first, then confusing, then a good idea but not realistic. The more we conform to its likeness, the more it is revealed that this Word not only makes sense but makes startling, magnificent sense. The Word corresponds to every yearning of our hearts, revealing that the Father has made for us a home with many rooms, with space for each of us.

9

What Can We Understand of Heaven for Souls Separated from Their Bodies?

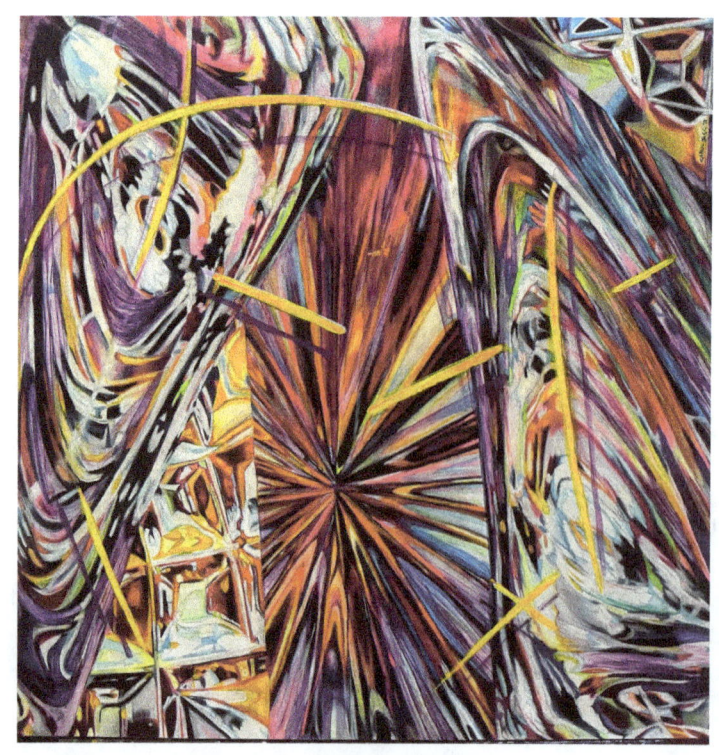

Split Apart, by Carol Scott

What Can We Understand of Heaven?

Today when I left, my soul anchored itself in the passing image, dredging the ocean floor
You glide across my surface, sleek unbroken thick impermeable line, pure reflective silver
In waveless water, life is not long, soundless song of my soul, it haunts and twists
This field of vision tunneling, felt not seen, edges of you in black jet night
Heightened luminescent core, your gravitational pull flowing from nowhere everywhere
I see the universe, your eyes my eyes, complex ecosystem, as above so below
The sense of being somewhere, somehow near, some intensity of you
As fragrance passed, through hair fallen waterfall, cascaded veil of shoulders stilled
Life is one long haunting, touching, peering through to the other side
The place I once was, cradlesong lullaby trace of me
You will and I will know you as you are, persistent . . .
I see the universe, your eyes my eyes, complex ecosystem, as above so below
Your complexion, a breviary of sacred prayer, codas of need, seen and felt
Candle read shadow, hymns and hours, psalm spoken lovers laying down, touching the other
Life my life my love, sing to me in your low tone, become the unearthed hum
The vibration of my heart
I did not know, my eyes, I did not know, these tears, I did not know, life is not long
Crystal ball tell us all, falling water wash us fresh, flies of fire play, make beauty
We grieve the dead, way of nature, forced, tides cannot be turned, flow with the flow
Persistence fades
I die to the universe, your eyes my eyes, complex ecosystem, as above so below

—"Today When I Left," by Carol Scott & Caitlin Smith Gilson

Our likening power gives us a unique dignity set apart from the angels. This longer way of time, embodiment, and fallible knowledge is its own gift. It places us relatively higher than the angels. Because of this, we must acknowledge that the state of the separated soul in heaven is *still* problematic. In heaven, God acts *in place* of our bodies, *in place* of how our ears can hear and conform to the Word. In heaven, God acts *in place* of our bodies, *in place* of how our hands can grasp the beloved, communicating love beyond words. In the state of the separated soul, God acts *in place* of our eyes so that we can see the truth, never turning away. God becomes the *in loco parentis* of our bodies. The Father does not bypass the gift of our likening power. His grace makes up for our lack of bodies, a lack due to sin, which caused death, a death unnatural to our natures. The state of the separated soul in heaven cannot be a place of quasi-inactivity. It cannot be merely the best memories of one's human life sustaining the soul. But without God acting *in place* of our bodies, no further experience is possible. The body is not present to provide the soul with the data—the sounds, sight, smells, touch, taste—that the soul takes in as knowledge. Once the soul understands what the body experiences, it entices the whole person, body and soul, to action. Heaven with no deepening of experience seems to be a state closer to hell than heaven. The soul stuck in the past without a chance to deepen is not even purgatory! Purgatory includes the gift to review the past and see truth. It allows us to acknowledge our sins. A separated soul trapped in what it was, unable to act on what it is now, is no heaven at all.

If God willed human souls to strain to attain knowledge in the same way that angels do, we would *not* achieve the clarity of angelic knowledge. Human knowledge would become unclarified, non-specific generalities. The human soul is not the right template to understand the eternal outside of time. The separated soul is not the right template to understand love without the specific experiences of love that occur in a human life. It is not the right foundation to understand truth without the various events in life that help us to arrive at truth. Could the soul endure knowledge without the body? Perhaps. But should this be its perfection? No. A thin, unwaxed paper cup given at the dentist for gargling is not the proper container for hot coffee. It may hold the coffee briefly, but the experience of it would be fraught with fear of spillage. It would be a distracted and caustic state, less perfect than its designed and intended use. This is the crisis of the state of the separated soul, which is so masked by the "better place" mantra. That masking only heightens the loss of faith. An empty heaven we cannot even envision is not the way to desire heaven. A heaven comprised of souls estranged from their bodies is not paradise. A heaven where we only have knowledge of our pasts or only vaguely understand universal generalities does not entice human hearts to believe with all their hearts and minds. The child killed prematurely deserves more than this kind of heaven. That child, who lit up everyone's lives with her smile, with the way she could throw the toy into the air and giggle triumphantly, is not made all the greater in such a deficient scenario of paradise. We desire the good of our bodies which God created for us. We want to see the child's smile, feel the softness of her cheek, and as God breathed into the nostrils of Adam to bring him to life, we want to see the child exhale the glories of a life truly redeemed.

How then do we authentically resolve this difficulty of the separated soul, one that influences every arena of human life? We have learned a number of intensifying but essential realities:

1. If heaven was a form of knowledge equivalent to the angels' direct turning to God, then we would be in an impasse. Heaven would not be a state of perfection for the human person. If heaven were a state where knowledge is *harder* to acquire because we are less capable of acquiring it, this would be plainly absurd! We are clearly walking a conceptual tightrope.

2. Faith and reason are not opposed; faith enables reason to gain humbling access into the mystery because, while beyond reason, the mystery is profoundly reasonable. We understand, by faith, that heaven is a state of the blessed, a state of perfection, that there is no lacking in heaven. This line must be held, and we must see how it *is* reasonable.

3. Paradoxically, we must acknowledge that the state of the separated soul of the blessed is both a concession to a nobler state and it contains no lacking either. If the concession is not present, then we are undermining that God intended human beings to be the unity of body and soul. We are ignoring that death tears this union apart, tears it apart like the seamless cloth. It is an unnatural separation resulting from sin and death. At the same time, to state that heaven is a place where something is lacking contradicts faith and contradicts reason's understanding that God is perfection itself. Nothing could be lacking when united to God. If heaven is seamless unity with God, no imperfection can be admitted.

God is Existence itself! It is not sufficient to call God *a* beautiful, or good, or true being as if these are each one of His additions. God does not possess a degree of these perfections. He is the uncreated and everlasting foundation of everything Good, True, and Beautiful. In fact, He is *identical with* Truth, Goodness, and Beauty. All perfections are directed to God, Who is all perfections:

> "Can any hide himself in secret places, that I shall not see him?" saith the LORD. "Do not I fill Heaven and Earth?" saith the LORD.
> —Jeremiah 23:34

God fills heaven and earth, and this truth must not be overlooked. We have always been yearning beings open to the divine reality that permeates and transcends the temporal and earthly. This is why for St. Paul heaven is our permanent home. Earth has never fully revealed our human nature because it *cannot*. The human person is a being in active *wait*. Both inwardly and outwardly, we seek the source of the meanings we experience in the world. Whereas the family dog enjoys warming her body in the sun, she cannot understand *why* it is enjoyable, and ask *how* the sun came to be or *when* it is completed. From our youngest age, when we, too, have enjoyed the sun and its warmth upon our backs, we have asked such questions. These questions begin in our experience of the world but require answers beyond it. The mystery of the human person is that we cannot know ourselves until we discover that the relationship between body and soul is the expression of a spiritual existence manifested in time. Even though we walk on earth, our souls stand before God. This is our nature as on the horizon between time and eternity. We can only discover ourselves in the presence of God.

God need not turn to nature or time as we do to learn, nor to the more exalted intellectual realities like the angels; none is appropriate for the Divine nature. God *is* Existence itself: every being in the line of createdness turns to Him to receive knowledge in varying modes and degrees, reflecting their natures. God is the Divine light, one simple indivisible First Principle. *By His own essence*, God knows all things. Instead of the body, the human person's separated soul turns to God. As Creator, God fills heaven and earth. Whereas no other created reality could appropriately take the place of our bodies in knowledge, God can authentically take the place of the body for us when in heaven. It is not good for us to grasp the eternal realities in the manner befitting the angels. This would fail to reflect the heaven God specifically intended for *human* beings. It would be a looking through the glass even more darkly than on earth. What use is the greatest sonata to the stone, or angelic knowledge to the human, or human carnality to the angel? We cannot square this circle. But the separated soul can turn to God. God is the Source and Perfection of all things and to which all things return. This is *most* fitting. Here, we retain the proper order that must not be bypassed. Faith is not magic but rigorous truth endowed with perfect love.

Still the concession must be present. Original sin was not necessary and was not what God intended. Death has generational consequences that are not removed by God perpetually taking the place of our bodies. The soul outlasts the body due to the disease of our sin, which removes the grace that held us from death. While heaven is surely without deficit, there is an integral directionality within that blessedness. We desire what God desires: we desire the resurrection. The resurrected state creates an anticipation and a purified yearning born not of emptiness or a will opposed to God's but of abundance and peace. This heavenly yearning comes from a quieted will, a will at rest, a will that is one with God's will. God eternally wills the Good for each of us. Our will rests in God's will. Unified, our wills are actively geared to the intimacy and singularity of each person's relationship with God. Each glorified body, even our vestments and walk and posture, communicate the perfected singularity of our relationship with God fulfilled to its unique perfection. Heaven becomes *more* of a community than any earthly version could ever achieve. Our likening power is fulfilled beyond our greatest dreams in the hope for the resurrection of our bodies.

All good communities seek to create genuine bonds as intimate as familial affection but universal beyond family lines. We seek a universal family. The history of human existence is a long effort, both noble and disastrous, to create civilizational families. We must seek to love our neighbors as ourselves, to love all. But to raise the word "love" beyond word play so that we can love *all* as our own is a goodness beyond our powers. A goodness we must seek but must acknowledge as greater than all of us. When the beloved dies and we react immediately with the "better place," let us be prepared to give that term its proper due. It functions to lessen the credibility of heaven if we leave the state of the separated soul as an unexamined, emptied bodiless presence. But the "better place" is realized in its astonishing dignity when we hope for our glorified bodies in the resurrected state. God takes the place of our bodies, the intimacy we sought on earth. He fulfills what we started when we first began to ask questions and to know ourselves. Our embodiment has always placed us in a conversation with God. In heaven, the conversation is now fulfilled. God makes up what sin and death caused us to lack. Original sin meant that our likening power to God was always cut short by disease, ignorance, vice, and death. If only we could enter the greatest reality of our image and likeness, then we could truly know and love others. Then we could fulfill the desire truly to love *all* with the intensity in which we love but a few. But death parts us. Before death are all the ways in which we lose our way and fracture families and community. There is no heavenly community on earth though we glimpse it in the best of family love. Even for the saintliest, death is parting. Our likening power that can bridge the division is halted, stunted. God takes the place of our bodies in heaven. This allows that conversation to be fulfilled that death prevented when it forcibly separated the soul from the body. But God in His goodness does not leave the end there. We have always sought love, love of the child, the friend, the spouse, God. We have sought the communion that cannot be fulfilled in bodies susceptible to sin, ignorance, disease, and death.

The hope for our glorified bodies is so very important and so worthy a desire. It enables us to participate in the universal family only dreamt on earth. Charles Péguy sets out what distinguishes us and elevates us above the angels. It is through Christ's flesh and blood that we will find our way home:

> The Franciscan Nun tells young Joan
> What those that are carnal lack, as we know, is being pure.
> But what we ought to know is that those that are pure lack being carnal.
> The angels are certainly pure, but they aren't the least bit carnal.
> They have no idea what it is to have a body, *to be* a body.
> They have no idea what it is to be a poor creature.
> A carnal creature.
> A body kneaded from the clay of the Earth.
> The carnal Earth.
> They don't understand this mysterious bond, this created bond,
> Infinitely mysterious,
> Between the soul and the body.
> This my child is what the angels do not understand.
> I mean to say, that this is what they haven't experienced.
> What it is to have this body; to have this bond with this body; to be this body,
> To have this bond with the Earth, with this Earth, to be this Earth, clay and dust, ash and the mud of the Earth,
> *The very body of Jesus.*
> —Charles Péguy, *The Portal of the Mystery of Hope*

10

No Man Is an Island

What Human Experience Teaches Us about Heaven

Gods and Fates, by Carol Scott

All This, and Heaven Too

When you sway the heavens and your head relaxes its weight
Falling back
All earth is lost forever, it slips inside your face
Reversed tears, every ounce inside your eyes

*I think you have gone to years before me
Young as bitten peach*

Half of you in distant light
The other in the ancient shade that once cast
The world into its first sleep
A puzzle of two pieces
You slip in and out of me
All I can do is breathe out my spirit
Finding the earth beneath your skin

Your life, your life, your passion
Your pleasure is sacred to me
This is the architecture of my longing
How can I survive?

You have made me from your tears
I am the sea of Galilee
The boats passing brightly
The catch in your nets
The damp of your lips
As the cup passes by, let the cup pass by
There is no pain here

Oh Holy Christ
There is the word of death and the word of life
The doors open, the windows
I will never close them
Come to me, beautiful song
Torched body, earth of you
I turn into wilderness in your fire

*I think you have gone to years before me
Young as bitten peach*

You affect my symmetry
The force of your life
I look at your face
Your face says it all

There is no earth
Your happiness is the holy
The earth is gone
Curve your back into the art of my hand
Wrapped completely
Downed world, dropped cut flowers
Your face veils the sky
Worlds in the broke open thigh
How can I survive?

Oh Holy Christ
The wheel of chance
The dance of death
Arch my back into the bridge of you
Before the world was made
It slipped inside your face
And I was the waking stream
Let the cup pass by, there is no pain here

I think you have gone to years before me
Young as bitten peach
    —"When You Sway the Heavens," by Caitlin Smith Gilson

All This, and Heaven Too

The unbroken thread in every human life: any act of experience places us simultaneously *inward* and *outward*. Inwardly, we enter through and beyond ourselves into our inner union with God. Outwardly, into the persons and places that situate us in life. It is never one or the other. All human experience places us within this dynamic, twofold yearning. This twofold structure stretches human persons beyond themselves. This is why memory is so powerful and poignant.

There is an invisible fabric, a netting, connecting each human person. Each of us is in conversation with the divine. And we are always in conversation with other persons who are *also* in conversation with the divine. Due to original sin, it takes us a long time to take the reality of a universal family seriously. We are more naturally bonded to others than isolated individuals. It is sin that separates us. Sin makes life fragmentary: we lose sight of the union we have *with* others, the responsibility we have *to* others. We suppress this universal thread linking us. It becomes easier to commit terrible sins when a person's relation to us is cut off.

No human person is a closed-up object as is a stone. The union of body and rational soul is a spiritual *tending*. Our bodies and souls allow us to experience, to be experienced, and to experience being experienced. We can experience the perfumed smell of the flower. Our friend can experience us enjoying the garden. We can realize, with a smile and a laugh, that our friend is enjoying watching us happily entranced among the roses. To be a human being involves layers of meaning and action. Every human life is in the midst of presences, persons, places, and relations. We interiorize not only our experiences but the experience of the other person who has experienced us. The more deeply we follow this thread, the closer we realize God is the root of it all. We realize that our intimacies in friendship and in love include an interiorization of the other person and an exteriorization of what we have taken in and contributed to the conversation. Each person is breathing in and out the presence of the other. Each time that spirit is breathed in, it mingles with one's own spirit and something both the same and new is exhaled, only to be inhaled again. We are bound up in the being of the other person so that grief is truly grief. The loss of the beloved is the seemingly impossible cutting away of ourselves, as it is the cutting off access to the loved one who has died. If we were not truly a universal family, if we were truly as the devil wants us—as fragmentary and isolated egos—grief would not have the devastating effect it does.

Let us suppose that we are nothing more than isolated egos. Let us pretend we are minds inside bodies who may or may not make connections with others. In this scenario, the connections made with others are fundamentally inessential. They are picked up and put down depending on some relative need or purpose, but not intrinsically who we are. In this scenario, the experience of relation to another person is something we may choose or lose, but not written into the very heart of our nature. The philosopher John Searle held this view. He sees human existence as akin to a multitude of brains in vats. The vat is the body that encases the nervous system. All humans are this structure. His view is that our brains are *all* we have for representing the world. We are brains in vats, the vat is a skull, and everything we call "persons" are the signals or messages impacting our nervous systems. How can grief have any place if we were merely brains in a vat taking in the disconnected messages that impact our nervous system?

What John Searle sets out couldn't be farther from the truth. It fails to reflect that inward and outward tending that characterizes all human interaction. It fails to grasp the meaning of our existence. Our existence precedes sensory data so that the information collected by our senses can be brought to our souls. Our souls have the capacity to reveal the meaning always present within those sense experiences. Meaning is always *more* than sensory experience. A brain in a vat has sense experiences without a netting of meaning, it has sound without word, color without masterpiece. The brain in the vat denies in advance that meaning underlies all human experience. If there is no meaning preceding sensory experience, connecting all experience, what exactly is derived when the senses experience something? Additionally, there is no soul to understand the experience as meaningful. A brain in a vat is a flood of data, not an experience. The *tending* structure inherent in all human acts must be acknowledged and respected.

Only by grasping this profound interconnectedness of human beings so shaped by our embodiment—by the touch of another, the sight that gives us context, the listening that places us in communion—can we encounter the magnificent and promised universal family in heaven. We have sought all along the great community, the beautiful embrace, the language that can be understood by all, the touch that conveys love so perfectly and truly, the kiss that truly can give peace.

The inward and outward experiences that constitute a human life are a robust acknowledgment that heaven could not be a disconnected, isolated experience. Nor could paradise consist of souls permanently severed from their bodies. When human beings learn, it is the capacity to take in the reality of the object, not merely to sense it. I can feel softness, see whiteness, but I *know* that these qualities are in the pillow, the rice, the marshmallow.

I can take in sensations and acquire the fundamental nature of the object. My soul differentiates objects that share similar sensory experiences. I can see and feel the fur of the small dog and the cat, I can hear each growling, I can experience similarities and differences, but knowledge is taking into my being what fundamentally characterizes each object, knowing it *as it is*. Even if the dog were to lose its fur, or the cat no longer growls, I understand what makes each its own. This capacity is yet another testament to the fabric where all of existence is interconnected. All human experience involves the taking in of things *as they are* and bringing these realities with us as we traverse life's journey. Grief occurs precisely because the loved one who has died is *still* very much present in us. The beloved is present in absence, present in memory, present as we begin making new memories. Sin perpetuates the illusion that human beings are isolated and disconnected, and that our actions do not affect other persons. We are in the image and likeness of God. Our participation means we achieve the permanence of knowledge, not the fleetingness of mere sensation. We know the tree as it is bare or full of fruit. We know the apple as it is fresh or as it is withered. We recognize the once-apple in the remaining seeds or the vague likeness of the apple in the abstract painting. We understand the apple in the allegory of the fall into sin. We are no mere brains in vats. Human knowledge involves the image of God. It involves bringing inwardly into permanent view what an object *is* in all its changes. We have the capacity in knowledge to see within created things their inward, interior divine source. We have the capacity to turn outwardly through sense experiences, to take in the world around us and bring it into shared participation with the eternal and everlasting. What a gift it is to see created things through our image in God! The human soul has the capacity to take in the world, to raise the things of the world into enduring meaning. We have the capacity to do so in *all* our relationships.

The worm may have a sensation of the apple but not a nucleus of self to know the apple in the many ways an apple can be present. The worm cannot know itself knowing and experiencing the apple, both when the apple is present and when it is long past being experienced. Even the smallest act of knowledge raises us above sensory experience and places us on the trajectory to desire heaven! Every act of knowledge seeks the dignity of permanence, of knowing the object, the other person, in all stages and manifestations. In knowledge, we retain what is long past its temporal presence. In human knowledge, we are *in* the world, *of* the world, and even *as* the world. We experience truth, we are experienced by others who seek knowledge, and we know ourselves as we are experienced by others. The human person has a unique participation in the world that unites sensation and knowledge, time and eternity, creation and the Creator. As things change, wither, and die, and we leave behind things, persons, events in our lives, all the same we never leave them, and they never leave us. To encounter them in the first place—not merely as the worm senses the apple but as a human being who *knows* the apple under many forms—necessitates that we achieve knowledge that is real, permanent, does not fade, and therefore has the eternal imprint upon it. Because knowledge has this dignity and power, no matter where we go, we do not leave behind the objects, places, and persons we have left or who have left us through death. This is why grief confounds us, breaks not only our hearts but stretches reason beyond itself. The beloved has left us and not left us all the same. And where do we go from there? There is only the hope for heaven . . .

We are all responsible *for* others because each of us is a result of responding to persons in such a way that our very temporality is altered. We see ourselves in the past, in shifting memories, in the anticipated future and our power to cultivate the future. This inward and outward relationality is not something we are able to choose or refuse. It naturally occurs by virtue of being ourselves in action. Recognizing this community of persons changes the understanding of what constitutes personhood. Our thought processes are not a compilation of vaguely defined egos, somehow independent and distinct. We are not brains in a vat receiving only sensory signals. Instead, what we call "our own thoughts" are always manifestly tied and bonded to others as inward towards God and outward to a community of human beings. This tending is a spiritual and familial scaffolding. We build the architecture of the world, foreshadowing the hope that, through Christ, we astonishingly co-design the architecture of paradise. This is one of the crucial gifts Christ gives us. When God became human, heaven visited earth, the eternal entered the temporal. Our experience of our humanity is brought into heaven, dramatically realized when Christ ascended.

Through our flesh and blood, we feel, taste, touch, smell, hear the manifold layers of the world. We take in the world and our soul elevates these sensations into knowledge. The unity of our body and soul gives us the unique capacity to see the dignity in all created things, the imprint of the eternal. We can see how love is a universal good *and* see how it is manifested as unrepeatable experiences throughout history. The loving friendship between Saints Claire and Francis reflects the permanence and eternality of love. It is also a unique experience never to be repeated. There are many companion experiences throughout history but never *exactly* the same. Our souls know the likeness and the difference. Our knowledge presents the divine reality in such a heartbreakingly beautiful way, it unveils the eternal *through* time. The anticipation of Christmas is a supreme example of this reality: Our Lady's *finite* womb carries the *infinite* promise, God Himself.

Only when we recognize this magnificent interconnectedness to human lives can we appreciate the gift of Christ. Christ complements and fulfills what our bodies and souls communicate. Christ offers His body and soul as the architecture of heaven and the *way* for us to hope for the resurrection of our bodies. Only when we experience that which lays at the center of our own soul as something that has always laid in the center of another can we glimpse how Christ's incarnation brought a glimpse of heaven to earth. The human soul is not something poured into the body, we are not brains in vats. Our lives are a conversation in how eternal and universal reality is deeply involved in the particularities of everyday life: time, memory, the great love affair, the missing beloved pet, the death of one child.

It is argued that a supreme God would not care about temporal things, would not be troubled by insignificant events in time. The indifference of God is incompatible with His simultaneous perfection and omniscience. The human person derives knowledge from temporal things. We understand eternal realities through changing things. God has great love of the temporal, finite, and daily things. God became human. Christ experienced and loved the temporal, finite, and daily things. When we catch sight of the temporal experience, when we see it *as* fleeting, this signifies a permanence within us. Things are changing around us and to us, but something within us stands immune to time to appreciate its embrace within experience. God has created a world in which the littlest things bring us to the Divine, the very conversation, every conversation, conveys the supreme interest of the Divine in the littlest things.

> Consider the lilies, how they grow: they toil not, they spin not; and yet I say unto you, that Solomon in all his glory was not arrayed like one of these.
> —Luke 12:27

Every human person carries the following clues to our hope for heaven:

A. All human questioning is a simultaneous twofold tending towards the Divine, inwardly and outwardly.

B. All human loves are a lifetime's interiorization and exteriorization of the beloved and the self.

Knowledge tends inwardly towards God and eternal reality and exteriorly towards the community of creatures, persons, event, places. Every daily question reflects this simultaneous twofold movement. "Is this choice good?" turns me to the interior depth beyond myself and my own powers to what truly constitutes goodness. It turns me outward beyond myself to the fabric of situations, persons, which must be addressed when examining whether a particular choice reflects the Good. This reality is expressed most dramatically in the union of the lover and beloved. Every lover is the beloved to the other. We as lovers take in far more than the sensory experience of our beloved. If it was only sensory experience, we wouldn't have love or even knowledge! We would be the worm having sensation of the apple but never knowing the apple. As best as we can, we interiorize what the beloved truly *is*. As lovers, we also take in the form of our own self that the beloved has, repeatedly in varying degrees, previously exteriorized. And the exteriorization of our self also includes a form of the beloved that has repeatedly over the years been interiorized and exteriorized by us, the lover. In the image and likeness of God, our experiences as lover and beloved involve, like Adam, coming alive through God's breath. We are a breathing in and out of the spirit, in which the dignity of that person, who that person *is*, is beyond measure and could never be satisfied with earthly things. The beloved carries all past, all time, and permeates all memory. This participates in the mystical depth of how once joined in marriage no person in this life can separate that union.

Our knowledge, experience, and love reveal a written-across-our-hearts hope for heaven. Our lives foreshadow the hope for Christ, who can complete the community that death cuts short. Christ completes the architecture we reveal in our relationships, which connects us always beyond ourselves. Human experience has always sought Christ's flesh and blood, which alone can complete the architecture of happiness we glimpse in the best of human relationships. We cannot fulfill this architecture alone, for we cannot make heaven on earth. Thankfully, Christ is the Bread of Life:

> Then Jesus declared, "I am the Bread of Life. Whoever comes to me will never go hungry, and whoever believes in me will never be thirsty."
> —John 6:35

Christ is one with heaven: "*I am the Way, the Truth, and the Life.*" Christ entered the world, descended into hell and made hell *real*. Remember that which runs away from God cannot make itself real. Christ alone realizes the magnitude of losing Christ and losing heaven. Then Our Lord resurrected in His glorified body to complete the transcendental Beauty of those inward and outward experiences of human life that connect us all. Death gravely and terminally interrupted this unity, but Christ restores its promise. How can we complete this full knowing of the beloved, how can we know ourselves, if death is the torn separation of the human person, the rupture of human experience? Christ's flesh completes what ours could not, it completes that inward and outward experience where we know ourselves and know the beloved.

> Ring in the love of truth and right,
> Ring in the common love of good.
> Ring out old shapes of foul disease;
> Ring out the narrowing lust of gold;
> Ring out the thousand wars of old,
> Ring in the thousand years of peace.
> Ring in the valiant man and free,
> The larger heart, the kindlier hand;
> Ring out the darkness of the land,
> Ring in the Christ that is to be.
> —Alfred Lord Tennyson, *In Memoriam*

We tend towards the Divine inwardly and outwardly, and through both we find Christ, resurrected with His opened wounds, as the revelation of that completed fabric of love. Christ is the supreme person who alone can help us fulfill ourselves. Our Lord not only completes in us what we have failed to complete but also gifts us with co-forming within His wounds the architecture of the church and family, the glimpses of heaven on earth. Through them we traverse the celestial architecture to come:

> Now I rejoice in my sufferings for you, and I am completing in my flesh what is lacking in Christ's afflictions for His body, that is, the church.
> —Colossians 1:24

> For my flesh is real food and my blood is real drink. Whoever eats my flesh and drinks my blood remains in me, and I in them. Just as the living Father sent me and I live because of the Father, so the one who feeds on me will live because of me. This is the bread that came down from heaven. Your ancestors ate manna and died, but whoever feeds on this bread will live forever.
> —John 6:56–58

11

A Glimpse of Hell

The Conscience of Failed Love

St. Paul's Moment, by Carol Scott

All This, and Heaven Too

Tunneling to the end if I lift my head what remains slams to the floor
Made of the matter of this and this, dead two years, hands on my face, on yours my palms Stretched fingering disbelief, nails as cleaned stone, your cheekbones rough as they were
And all our tears cannot unlearn the path of descent, you have been pulled out from beneath me, There is too much of the uprooted ground for the earth to tilt back it cannot save
Powerless you come, a gaze without sight, every look replete with agony, clothed as you were, Made of the matter and the mind, Devoured in the infinite wreath of things to come
Can we not collide, stash our souls into the other and survive the last temptation
Love cannot be this and this, for you shadowing you, peeled film cascading
The coverall of weeping child
Can we not collide, made of might and star, your eyes the resigning feature
The doorway subsiding, Christ in far off land, and my sorrow trawls into the deep
We are made of the weak, each heart weaker than the next . . .
If only we could live and be and forward the earth into permanent futurity
Skin of geometric dimensions folding into sweetest candy, to catch wisdom with painted sugar
Falling from the sky as rain, rain in rundown suns, thousands of suns
Stepping lighter into the clouds, one day we will jump to the top
To the terracotta tiles that cover the church roof, lighter than air and sliding down
Becoming a slope of snow in the Alps, my Lord you pulled the rug out from beneath me
Oh, we flow until we dry into ash, undo the die that has been cast
This weakest love weakening me, and all our tears cannot unlearn the path of descent

 —"My Father," (excerpt) by Caitlin Smith Gilson

> Cain, sleeping not, dreamed at the mountain foot. Raising his head, in that funereal Heaven he saw an eye, a great eye, in the night open, and staring at him in the gloom. "I am too near," he said, and tremblingly woke up his sleeping sons again, and his tired wife, and fled through space and darkness. Thirty days he went, and thirty nights, nor looked behind; pale, silent, watchful, shaking at each sound; no rest, no sleep, till he attained the strand.
> Where the sea washes that which since was Asshur.... "Is the Eye gone?" ... Cain replied: "Nay, it is even there." Then added: "I will live beneath the Earth, as a lone man within his sepulcher. I will see nothing; will be seen of none." ... But when he sat, so ghost-like, in his chair, and they had closed the dungeon over his head, the Eye was in the tomb and fixed on Cain.
> —Victor Hugo, "La Conscience"

THERE IS A UNIQUE netting where each person is deeply connected to others and sin has long since clouded that reality and its obligations. Now, we take a glimpse at the kind of conscience that has the power to conjure a glimpse of hell. Human beings can potentially refuse God completely and terminally. What kind of conscience would this terrible state have if it *can* be described? In Victor Hugo's poem, Cain and his family have attempted to disconnect the connection to God at root in all human experience. But because this *connectedness* is inescapable, Cain is haunted by the reality of God in every choice he makes and every relation he has. He attempts to sever the bonds to preserve himself. Instead, he unravels his very personhood. This interconnectedness will only return as a haunting reality. Cain attempts to sever the relationships that make us. But we are always bound up in the lives and memories of other human beings all standing under God. The tomb symbolizes Cain's spiritual and ethical emptiness. It shows the terrible state of his personhood confronted by the faces, especially God's watchful eye, which he failed to escape. The tomb is his guilty conscience. Cain attempts to make his personhood *outside* of the relationships that always point to the Divine, to heaven as permanent home. In doing so, this uproots his human nature. How can he remember without the context of others? How can Cain anticipate the next steps without the fabric of what other persons bring to his life? His refusal to know himself within a true community under God curls his own timeline back upon himself, creating another kind of time. He is deforming into a static glacier of anti-eternity. Cain is causing the hellish torn separation of his soul from his body *before* his death! In his refusal to acknowledge the responsibility of his personhood, he has dissolved any access to true freedom. God's ever-following eye is viewed as threat for Cain. But those who do desire the spiritual community understand the divine gaze as the loving invitation to God. Cain refuses to address his responsibilities or stretch himself towards other persons. He and his tribe run from the very sight needed to know and love truly.

Cain's efforts to build walls, cities, cultures against God are not unlike the attacks on traditional Western culture that demand the death of the family and church. But there is no remolding or making of a utopia on the rubble of a so-called post-Christian world. No matter where Cain travels, the eye follows and remains with him, even seeking him out within the tomb. His disintegration is his own doing, as hell is always our own choice.

Cain trapped himself in an unchangeable rigidity. He prevents the desire for conversion and forgiveness. Today, we see this ideological rigidity as precursor to hell in the many forms of failed conscience. Below are four forms of failed conscience. In different ways, the human person denies, obscures, wounds, and even razes to the ground his relationship with God, persons, and himself. Each form of failed conscience represents aspects of hell realized on earth. They also reveal the twilight of Christ within the culture. Our fourth form, *the conscience of failed love,* carries with it profound layers of suffering. It still has access to human relationships that are salvific rather than damning and will be given the most attention. To encounter and appreciate how heaven fulfills our nature, how genuine relationships have *always* been an inkling of our paradisal home, we must, with Christ, descend a little into the earthly hells. These are the glimpses of hell we have created by our self-imposed exile from God.

The Fraudulent Conscience

The fraudulent conscience is reserved for those who give a great deal of thought to how they are perceived while sidestepping any redemptive sense of goodness. They shirk the idea of being viewed as callous, conscience-less, or cowardly. These views would render them naked and expose their state of shallowness. There is a recognition of the proper human nature and genuine community with others, but it is always viewed as a troublesome pursuit. The fraudulent conscience pantomimes a sense of relationship, a "going through the motions" as the way to outwit death and confirm one's legacy. This failed conscience does not possess the ability to bear the true gaze and contributions of other persons. This is a foreshadowing of hell as self-alienation.

In Plato's *Gorgias*, we meet Polus, the flatterer. He is the sycophantic student of the notable rhetorician Gorgias. We see Polus embody the fraudulent conscience in his embarrassing defense of his teacher. Polus admonishes Socrates for bad form by not following the unwritten rules of civil society. Socrates should not have raised the question as to whether the rhetorician could and should teach justice. For Polus, it is an inappropriate and impolite question. It is aimed to hurt; no sensible civil educator would ever deny knowing justice or fail to teach it! Everything for Polus is decoration and trappings. Polus accuses Socrates of manipulating Gorgias into a corner when asking Gorgias to defend his good values. For Polus, this is in poor taste on the part of Socrates.

Towards the end of their exchange, Socrates gets the upper hand on Polus. Polus cannot bear the gaze of Socrates nor the genuine obligations to truth expected in their discussions. Socrates gets Polus openly to agree that rhetoric would *only* be good if it helped to enable the guilty to accuse himself and to seek his punishment. But rhetoric is often used to circumvent justice and help the criminal secure gains from injustice. Gorgias and Polus are sought after for their advice on how to deceive and outwit justice. Polus cannot reconcile his desire to appear noble and virtuous while committed to a fraudulent conscience. Polus cannot publicly deny that Socrates's conclusions follow from the premises. The results are absurd and secretly contrary to the very aims of his "art" or profession. Polus is embarrassed not by his conscience but merely by the sting of defeat. He is bound to the so-called rules of "polite" society to agree with Socrates that his profession should *only* encourage the guilty to confess. Socrates tricked Polus and outplayed him at his own game. The just man who looks guilty for Polus is foolish and in a worse position than the unjust man who appears just. As a fraudulent conscience, Polus pantomimes agreement with Socrates to satisfy the appearance of justice. He agrees with Socrates that the guilty should be the first to accuse themselves of misdeeds and should use rhetoric for the sole purpose of exposing their own evils. To appear just, Polus unwittingly exposes himself as a fraud.

The Parasitical Conscience

The parasitical conscience is a predatory form of relationship. It is also a strange and unnerving form of conscience, being the most honest with respect to its condition. The parasitical conscience recognizes itself for what it is. This failed conscience understands the power of forming perspectives and the place of opinions in manipulating others. The parasitical conscience recognizes the value of relationships as the demons are among the first to recognize Christ. This failed conscience decides to create a predatorial form of relationship with other persons. We realize ourselves in relation to others. The parasitical conscience subsumes other persons. It cuts off the possibility of self-knowledge and alienates persons out of existence. This conscience replaces relationship and community with a parasitical dimension. This conscience only exists by feeding on others; it is a host and vector entrapment. It foreshadows hell through the diminishing returns of unraveled friendships, unions, and partnerships. We see this terrible conscience in Sartre's famous tragedy *No Exit*. The character of Inez lives to make others suffer. She becomes the mirror for the others, but what she reflects sucks the life out of them. She has become such a spiritual parasite that her lifeforce depends entirely on destroying another:

> When I say I'm cruel, I mean I can't get on without making people suffer. Like a live coal. A live coal in another one's heart. When I'm alone I flicker out. For six months I flamed away in her heart, till there was nothing but a cinder. One night she got up and turned on the gas while I was asleep. Then she crept back into bed. So now you know.
> —Jean-Paul Sartre, *No Exit*

The Shallow Conscience

We often think there is little threat from those without reflective depth and exuding shallowness. But those with a surface-level conscience present a great danger. This is an almost conscienceless disposition by virtue of the failure to think. This person does not give even a first glance to any actions beyond himself. He does not think in terms of a struggle or acknowledgment of conscience as the others do. The fraudulent Polus may fail in conscience but has reflected on how it should "look." The parasitical Inez is indifferent to her own failure but knows well what happens to those around her because of her choices. But the shallow conscience is something different altogether. Usually, human desire and relationships are reflective. We must turn inwardly to our conscience and outwardly towards others when making moral decisions. This is how we enact our conscience. But a vacant conscience has instinctively avoided the reflective demands of human relationships. It refuses both inward and outward reflections. This failed conscience has codified its pure unexamined desires. It *never* engages personal reflection, which develops conscience. Such a person desires, as if without thought, the continuation of his or her desire to be desired. To be desired *is* the sole desire. This conscience is at ease with becoming an object for others as long as that ever-forward desire remains intact. This is Kierkegaard's parable of the "vain and wanton woman" whose use of the reflective mirror is not a parable for human communion but the very opposite. It is not a window to the soul. This mirror is the opposite of conscience, it is pure conscienceless appearance reflected, unexamined shallow desire. This failed conscience has the least depth and yet this poses little problem for it hasn't been given any thought. To do so would be to lessen that pure desire, to open it to the examination of conscience, and to stop the forward movement of being desired. But again, such a conscience hasn't given the situation any thought. A shallow unreflective conscience is the perfect template for political upheaval and for cultural discord and disintegration. Today, we see it everywhere, under the banners of woke ideology. It is a lethal dose performed while asleep. Hell marches forward and intoxicates the soul with an unknowing, shallow, and unreflective acceptance.

The Conscience of Failed Love: Long Day's Journey into Night

The three previous failed forms of conscience create precursors to the self-alienation in hell. There is no legacy of love in relationships with others; there is an absence of good desire for others. These consciences are irremediably cruel and approach something of the "un-person" found in the metaphysics of the satanic. Personhood necessitates *positive* relationships with others. If *all* our relationships are one of these failed forms, we glimpse the "un-person" quality of the damned.

What about the conscience that *tends* towards love but in failed ways, in partial truths, in lies hoping to bring about good ends? This failed conscience revolves around families. Heaven is embodied in the Holy Family. Paradise captures the pulse and heart of all happy families. The desire for heaven is in the aching reality of all unhappy families. It is felt in neglect and ruin when we still seek to love and hope. What shines forth in the Holy Family is the Trinitarian unity. Each person is knitted into the other, united interiorly and exteriorly. As the Father reveals Himself *as Father* through the Son, each member of the family has this profound interconnectedness. The glory of heaven streams forth. Heaven visits earth in the child, as Christ accomplished through His incarnation. This is the model of the family to which we are invited.

We must tread carefully examining the conscience of failed love. Unlike the prior three failed forms of conscience, this one genuinely desires the good for others. It is where the most heartbreaking glimpse of hell and the hope for heaven meet. We anchor our discussions in Eugene's O'Neill's veiled autobiographical tragedy *A Long Day's Journey into Night*. In this play, we have a family as failing image of the Holy Family. By "failing" we do not mean the fraudulent, parasitical, or shallow variants, which willfully defect from our image and likeness. Instead, we are in the presence of a family that craves with disquieting sadness the good relationship but fails in their spiritual resources. They obscure their likeness to the Holy Family. Even the play's opening dedication from Eugene O'Neill to his wife Carlotta reflects this tragic loss:

> For Carlotta, on our twelfth Wedding Anniversary: Dearest, I give you the original script of this play of old sorrow, written in tears and blood. A sadly inappropriate gift, it would seem, for a day celebrating happiness. But you will understand. I mean it as a tribute to your love and tenderness which gave me the faith in love that enabled me to face my dead at last and write this play—write it with deep pity and understanding and forgiveness for all the four haunted Tyrones. These twelve years, Beloved One, have been a Journey into Light—into love. You know my gratitude. And my love! Gene, Tao House, July 22, 1941.
> —Eugene O'Neill, *Long Day's Journey into Night*, dedication

O'Neill's Tyrone family confused the shadows with proper image and likenesses. But even shadows bear resemblances to God. What is striking is that Mary Tyrone, the mother, reflects failing and flailing love; she is the center of that family. Mary Tyrone still reflects a yearning for Our Lady, for the Holy Mother as source that knits the family together. The Tyrone family has their matriarch as the mediatrix of their desired redemption.

> In the practical proportions of human history, we come back to that fundamental of the father and the mother and the child. It has been said already that if this story cannot start with religious assumptions, it must none the less start with some moral or metaphysical assumptions, or no sense can be made of the story of man. . . . If we are not of those who begin by invoking a divine

Trinity, we must none the less invoke a human Trinity; and see that triangle repeated everywhere in the pattern of the world.
—G. K. Chesterton, *The Everlasting Man*

Long Day's Journey into Night is a foretaste of hell. It is a looking glass through to the estranged heaven within the many "might have beens" that characterize all human life. Hidden within the hours of one languishing day, we experience incomplete and partial love. These loves inaugurate the dissolution of the family and attempt the art of survival. The four main characters are heartrendingly filled with aspects of genuine love for their family. There is heartfelt concern and a desire for the good of the other. This is a unique family, but its story is founded in countless families across time and history. We have James Tyrone or Tyrone, the father; Mary, the mother; Jamie, the eldest son; and Edmund, the youngest son, born after the death of their middle child, who died of measles at age two. The whole tragedy is failing love interlaced with goodwill and lies, blame, guilt, and shame. Each family member has love interlaced with unresolved guilt. Each uses lies as protective cover, directed towards each other member. Each self-loathes and self-punishes while loathing and punishing and yet loving the other. Mary, for example, blames young Jamie for entering the child's room when he had measles. She blames the husband for always skimping on costs for medical treatments. She loves Edmund but nevertheless looks at him with guilt, as the accident, the replacement for the unreplaceable child. Most of all, and with a relentless quiet destruction, she blames herself. If only she had kept her guard up, had not become comfortable leaving the child in the care of others, he would not be dead.

Crucially, there are still *positive* aspects towards each of the family members, which were absent in the prior three forms of failed conscience. In this long day, we have a far more frightful version of hell on earth. This is hell not of the absence of love but of its failed form. The Tyrone family are seeking to recover their transcendent value. Each is bound to the lives of the other members of the family through love, memory, time, and history. But the threads unravel as quickly as they can be stitched together. Each member is the person-dissolving force for the self and for the other family members. Edmund loses the very hope that keeps him in *positive* relation with others. He has placed the fulfillment of his personhood in the *other* family members, who cannot love themselves or bear the gaze of the other person. Edmund cannot endure his selfhood derived from them. If only his mother would keep to her drug rehabilitation; if only her glassy, dissociating look is not what he knows it to be. Why won't the mother gaze at him with redeemed love and through her he will be redeemed? The facade begins to break. He asks her, "What can I believe?" to which Mary responds:

> Nothing, I don't blame you. How could you believe me—when I can't believe myself? I've become such a liar. I never lied about anything once upon a time. Now I have to lie, especially to myself. But how can you understand, when I don't myself. I've never understood anything about it, except that one day long ago I found I could no longer call my soul my own. *She pauses—then lowering her voice to a strange tone of whispered confidence.* But some day, dear, I will find it again—some day when you're all well, and I see you healthy and happy and successful, and I don't have to feel guilty any more—some day when the Blessed Virgin Mary forgives me and gives me back the faith in Her love and pity I used to have in my convent days, and I can pray to Her again—when She sees no one in the world can believe in me even for a moment any more, then She will believe in me, and with Her help it will be so easy. I will hear myself scream with agony, and at the same time I will laugh because I will be so sure of myself. *Then as Edmund remains hopelessly silent, she adds sadly.* Of course, you can't believe that, either. *She rises from the arm of his chair and goes to stare out the windows at right with her back to him—casually.*
> —Eugene O'Neill, *Long Day's Journey into Night*

To be a person is this intrinsic relationship fully realized in love. Personhood is our twofold *tending*, inward into the self, into the heart of God, and outward towards others *and* to the heart of God. We uncover ourselves through the relationships we have with each other. There is no stabilized innate nucleus to each person that exists outside communion and relationship. This is the drama and danger of human existence, the precariousness of humanity. The power of human bonds can elevate or annihilate the other person. This precariousness is what Eugene O'Neill unveils. Human persons never persist in their own isolated mode of thinking. Our beings are always in dynamic conversation with others from the moment they exist. This is why all human virtues and vices exist as shared and pardoned through Christ's humanity. Christ is the salvific fulfillment of love and communion. Unfailing love is united to eternity and responsibility. Love at its highest, deepest, truest, and most beautiful is, with Boethius, *"The complete and perfect possession of unending life."*

When we love, we seek the best for the beloved. We do not desire the temporary or the perishable, but the enduring and perfecting happiness that will fulfill the loved one. By loving, we embody true eternity for the other person. The beloved unveils goodness for us as we seek to do the same. Because we must find our image and likeness to God through persons and community, we intensify that divine image each time we interiorize and exteriorize ourselves in the exchange of love and compassion with the beloved. To think of myself in heaven without my children and my husband would cease to be heaven altogether. I would not be in heaven. Who I am is wholly bound up in the gifts and love they brought into me and formed my personhood by their lives. I have become who I am in that twofold interiorization and exteriorization that they helped accomplish. I would not be *this* person without them, and they would not be *their* persons without me. This is the radical truth of the human relationship and its song and its poetry. The Tyrone family have pinned their hopes on the others who comprise their family nucleus. While they have the genuine desire for the heavenly family, they cling to each other in a dissolving and damaging way. They choose the perishable, the lie, the kindly deceit, the denial that shifts responsibility. These are the vehicles of destruction and the mode of expression for their family love.

The Tyrone family have a very specific, partial, and corrupt view of eternal life, love, and happiness. But their views are also a testament to the universal fallen condition. As readers, we experience our own failed unions. We uncover our spiritual woundedness with every instance of love and happiness they express for the other. We cannot meaningfully persist without seeking the happiness of the beloved. We witness how their spiritual appetites survive because they seek goodness even amid all the lies. Helplessly, we watch as each member is given enough spiritual food to reanimate that desire for heaven. Each time it is cut down in all the wrong avenues undertaken in the name of love. The Tyrones attempt to claim responsibility for themselves, and for the others. They partially recognize their failures to bear things through, turning to alcohol and drug abuse, to escape the gaze of themselves and their family members. There is no monster lurking in the corner of that summer house to explain the failures. There is no sinister plot deforming that long day into night. We cannot pin all the failure and all the injustice on some evil *outside* the union of their failed loves. Solzhenitsyn describes this haunting reality cutting through the heart of each human being. Each person reflects the fallen state for themselves and for others. We are all in wounded likeness to the Holy Family:

> If only there were evil people somewhere insidiously committing evil deeds, and it were necessary only to separate them from the rest of us and destroy them. But the line dividing good and evil cuts through the heart of every human being. And who is willing to destroy a piece of his own heart? During the life of any heart this line keeps changing place; sometimes it is squeezed one way by exuberant evil and sometimes it shifts to allow enough space for good to flourish. One and the same human being is, at various ages, under various circumstances, a totally different human being. At times he is close to being a devil, at times to sainthood. But his name doesn't change, and to that name we ascribe the whole lot, good and evil. . . . Socrates taught us: "Know thyself." Confronted by the pit into which we are about to toss those who have done us harm, we halt, stricken dumb: it is after all only because of the way things worked out that they were the executioners and we weren't. From good to evil is one quaver, says the proverb. And correspondingly, from evil to good.
> —Aleksandr Solzhenitsyn, *The Gulag Archipelago*

Each Tyrone has good intentions that extend each day and recede back into failure as evening draws close. They are exhausted by hopes they cannot fulfill, painfully reanimated at the start of each day. Each feels a far-off sense of liberation that lingers in the air and draws them into bondage. Every day is the promise of resurrection and the descent into hell. They hold each other captive but not out of lovelessness and cruelty. They are imprisoned by failed love and a commitment to the other drowning in lies. They are entrapping themselves at the threshold of hell. Each Tyrone fights against the loss of their collective personhoods but with spiritually insufficient tools. They now only love each other by avoiding at all costs the penetrating gaze into the self and into the other family member. If they do, what they see as true must dissolve and become lie; it must not, *cannot*, reveal the truth. We see this terrible denial when Edmund cannot admit to himself that his mother is abusing morphine again:

> *Frightenedly—with a desperate hoping against hope*
> He's a liar! It's a lie, isn't it, Mama?
> *Keeping her eyes averted.*
> What is a lie? Now you're talking in riddles like Jamie.
> *Then her eyes meet his stricken, accusing look. She stammers.*

> Edmund! Don't!
> *She looks away and her manner instantly regains the quality of strange detachment—calmly.*
> —Eugene O'Neill, *Long Day's Journey into Night*

The Tyrones are children of Cain, entombing themselves as the Eye pursues them. Human love is at the heart of this tragedy. Every failure to remain *remains* within us as a failure to remain. Something more sacred, lonelier, and wild remains. Shifting between person-dissolution and relentless efforts to undo that disintegration, something nevertheless *must* remain. They seek to redeem themselves and the other family members *as* they are being torn apart, dissolved. The love in them that makes them a family remains—remains as failure, remains as memory, remains as heartache, but remains stained, grafted, transposed, and transfixed within their flesh and blood. It remains in a form muted, muffled, unable to be extracted in any sense of undiluted goodness. We, like them, stumble around excavating within ourselves the tiresome litany of wrong words and wrong timing. Stubborn and fighting for survival, this hollowed out failing love still enables the Tyrones to retain ghosts of personhood within their collective dissipation. We witness, particularly through Edmund, the family ties that act out our original sin. We are with Edmund walking into the fog where he can longer see the house, no longer recognize the family bonds, where everything can hide within itself as if ghosts can take refuge inside ghosts:

> The fog was where I wanted to be. Halfway down the path you can't see this house. You'd never know it was here. Or any of the other places down the avenue. I couldn't see but a few feet ahead. I didn't meet a soul. Everything looked and sounded unreal. Nothing was what it is. That's what I wanted—to be alone with myself in another world where truth is untrue, and life can hide from itself. Out beyond the harbor, where the road runs along the beach, I even lost the feeling of being on land. The fog and the sea seemed part of each other. It was like walking on the bottom of the sea. As if I had drowned long ago. As if I was the ghost belonging to the fog, and the fog was the ghost of the sea. It felt damned peaceful to be nothing more than a ghost within a ghost.
> —Eugene O'Neill, *Long Day's Journey into Night*

These ghosts of personhood are a danger to the redemptive love that paradoxically helped form them. This wounded family unveils ghosts of the past that afflict and will not lay buried. There are phantoms of an unbearable present knocking about upstairs, and specters of a future unworthy of anticipation. The Tyrones' tortured temporality is created by their bonds fighting to survive the lies and to redeem the family. But these ghosts are as much phantasm as fantasy. These ghosts are woven by semblances of truth and persistent lies that degrade what remains into shadowy semblances. In this family of failed love, we recognize in each of us the marriage of lies and truth. It is why the lights must be lowered, why eyes must be averted, why water must replace the dwindling whiskey in the decanter, why confrontations are only made in detachment and anger or drunkenness, in any manner that can obscure the truth.

"Mechanically," is used several times throughout the play. This is in sharp contrast to the raw and primal desires that dominated the dialogue. This gives us an illusion that each family member has surrendered the tools to fight the lies that overtake them. In essence, their hands are lopped off but still grasping for their weapon of choice. The Tyrone men are perhaps terminally wounded, but they are still grasping for hope—impossible, absurd hope. The three men hinge everything on Mary somehow not relapsing back into addiction. If Mary survives and accomplishes sobriety, something she has never once completed, they see her triumph as saving them. Their fraught relationship with her keeps each of them afloat. Through hope for Mary's cure, each Tyrone reflects a glimmer of *positive* relationality. Her victory means the Tyrone men could survive and become something *more* substantial. As if Mary could bring each of them out of the abyss. As if this "happily ever" is not the wish of fools, the aged, and the dying but the deep wish for paradise. With the eldest son, Jamie:

> I suppose it's because I feel so damned sunk. Because this time Mama had me fooled. I really believed she had it licked. She thinks I always believe the worst, but this time I believed the best.
> *His voice flutters.*
> I suppose I can't forgive her—yet. It meant so much. I'd begun to hope, if she'd beaten the game, I could, too.
> *He begins to sob, and the horrible part of his weeping is that it appears sober, not the maudlin tears of drunkenness.*
> —Eugene O'Neill, *Long Day's Journey into Night*

Each Tyrone has unified the impossible: truth and lies. They are chimeras of failed love, relentlessly heading towards love *and* failure. O'Neill has portrayed this family thrown spiritually overboard in the storm. They are in the middle of the swollen ocean, clinging to the other, but oh how they cling! They are the others' life preserver and, more secretly, their anchor. Each drags the other down into the depths. Furiously, they grasp hold, seeking genuinely the life preserver of the other's love, still present by way of fallen forms. The Tyrones grasp each other with such terrifying force. They have each reckoned with the possibility that if one of them was eternally lost—lost in hell—then they would be unable to love completely. They instinctually recognize that something irremediable and unrecoverable would enter their hearts and every place where spirit dwells if the other sinks down beyond reach.

Their family relationship is an uneasy union of truth and lies. Each family member is for the other the weighted chain that drags them down. Jamie's drunken speech to his brother, warning him that he seeks his downfall, admits as much. It is a warning. It is truth *as love* but wrapped in drunkenness, which causes his warning to be set aside by Edmund as nonsense and falsehood. Edmund believes he mustn't give this nonsense a second thought. He must do so to survive the family structure of lies and failed loves. We feel the core of original sin inherited by us all. The truth must be sidestepped for love's sake. For God's sake, if one is to say the truth, package it in tomfoolery, in ways that present it as untruth, a dismissible foolishness. More gravely, make the truth act as a lie. When the Tyrones finally speak the truth, they enact a vice, never permitting the truth to be communicated *as truthful*:

> What I wanted to say is, I'd like to see you become the greatest success in the world. But you'd better be on your guard. Because I'll do my damnedest to make you fail. Can't help it. I hate myself. Got to take revenge. On everyone else. Especially you. . . . The dead part of me hopes you won't get well. Maybe he's even glad the same has got Mama again! He wants company, he doesn't want to be the only corpse around the house! *He gives a hard tortured laugh.*
> Jesus Jamie! You really have gone crazy!
> Think it over and you'll see I'm right. Think it over when you're away from me. . . . Tell people, "I had a brother, but he's dead." And when you come back, look out for me. I'll be waiting to welcome you with that "old pal" stuff, and give you the glad hand, and at the first good chance I get stab you in the back.
> Shut up! I'll be God-damned if I listen to you any more—
> *As if he hadn't heard.* Only don't forget me. Remember I warned you— for your sake. Give me credit. Greater love hath no man than this, that he saveth his brother from himself. *Very drunkenly, his head bobbing.*
> —Eugene O'Neill, *Long Day's Journey into Night*

To survive the heartaches, the losses, and the disappointments, we put on masks. To endure the demeaning comparisons, the armory of inflicted suffering, the ugliness, we put on masks. This is the face, the countenance, the persona that aligns more often with appearance than reality. It protects us from the penetrating gaze of others. But it damages our sense of moral obligation and *positive* relationships. The fragility of our image and likeness to God is within the midst of this mask. The longshot hope is that if we must put on a mask, which appears necessary for worldly survival, it is virtuous and transcendent, so we become what it portrays. We put on the mask of goodness and by interiorizing and exteriorizing it, the face becomes us. We are sublimated into its goodness, and we in turn speak its transcendent love in all we do. But we can also put the mask of lies on. We *think* we remain in control and can take the mask on and off, dangerously balancing reality and illusion, the person and the persona. This will infirm our souls in the process. We interiorize and exteriorize this mask of vice until we are unsure whether we'd survive without it. Terror seeps into us. How could we survive without those close caresses that brush aside reality? Has it all become too indistinguishable, the truth from the lies? Has the soul gone too far? Have we even forgotten that the mask is on? Life has come between us and what we would like to be, that we may have become lost forever.

> But I suppose life has made him like that, and he can't help it. None of us can help the things life has done to us. They're done before you realize it, and once they're done they make you do other things until at last everything comes between you and what you'd like to be, and you've lost your true self forever.
> —Eugene O'Neill, *Long Day's Journey into Night*

In *Long Day's Journey into Night*, each family member has a mask:

1. to keep the family love intact through meals together, drink, camaraderie, living room conversations, the intimate pleasantries of family life.
2. to protect themselves from the haunting truths that will erode family bonds.

These masks foreshadow hell. The Tyrone family wear masks to keep pleasantries and love alive while avoiding Mary's morphine abuse; her resentfulness regarding Jamie's hand in the death of Eugene; her regret over having another child, Edmund; her wishing Edmund had never been born; Edmund's disease that might kill him; Jamie's resentfulness of living in his brother's shadow in the family; Jamie's resentfulness of living in his father's shadow professionally; James Tyrone's guilt for selecting the cheap treatment that promoted his wife's addiction. The list of shame and lies goes on. It is either overcome in heaven or is the very stuff of hell. But it depends on whether they can remove the masks and love truthfully.

What happens when the masks are removed in the Tyrone family? Especially when each mask has fastened itself to the face, fused itself to the flesh, used the blood vessels to supply the mask with color, contour, and texture? How can it be pulled apart without destroying the bearer underneath? What happens when this union of failed loves is interiorized and exteriorized repeatedly? It becomes a vicious substitute for our image and likeness to God. It controls fate and futures and doubles as spiritual stagnation and deadening indecision. When family members exteriorize their masks for the other member, offering defected love, they receive in return the same failed love to interiorize. Each Tyrone exteriorizes and interiorizes boundless fear, self-loathing, and unresolved regret, repeatedly hidden and brushed aside to protect pleasantries and family bonds. Where can the good be found in such a circumstance? Faith is not magic. Where is the inkling of heaven on earth found in flesh, from God to humanity?

We can create signatures of hell on earth, thresholds of damnation in the very family unit. This speaks more to the promise of heaven within the worn patina of earth than to its denial as irrelevant and antiquated. This anguish, this ability for us to fuse the false mask, is the beginning of hell for our ruptured personhood. The masks reflect our intrinsic supernatural destiny even if they reflect it by defection. Heaven is the only satisfying home. We are not purely material beings directed towards purely material ends. The supernatural depths we descend when squandering our spiritual food are startling and terrifying.

The two goals of the mask, keeping the Tyrone family together while hiding haunting primal truths, have dueled with each other perhaps for too long. Now, redemption may have no place, no avenue left to conquer the soul. Their failed love has created a hellish, chimerical being, where "the true self is lost forever." This is the torn separation of the soul from the body and it happens here in our person. Christ realized this awful power when He descended into hell. Hell can begin on earth. We witness it in the consciences of failed loves. The Tyrones' willingness to lie and to delude themselves to protect family bonds breeds the simmering undercurrent of truth *as* resentfulness. Their love is unable to be seen *as* inviting, *as* good.

All This, and Heaven Too

This is the potentially terminal problem of the Tyrone family. The swirling miasma of lies to protect love has enshrined a love that is both present and absent. *Present*—for they love each other, that's precisely what prompted the lies! They sought ways to avoid pain and to rewrite history, not only for themselves but also for their family members. *Absent*—because they encased and entombed love in lies, failing repeatedly to love completely, fully, honestly, authentically. Love is now the seething undercurrent that bursts at the seams from every character who utters truth and then apologizes for his angered, drunken, drugged out, unacceptable, and vitriolic remarks. They make the telling of truth the enemy of truth-telling. The irony is that the characters apologize for the truth. They ask forgiveness for the goodness impossibly packaged in destruction. They end up giving love that does not have the ability to heal, transform, and redeem!

Genuine truth and love have been suppressed by their masks. They only reveal themselves as alienation and resentfulness, taking on the appearance of the opposite of truth and love! What they desire are the very things they suppress in their desires. This resentfulness is in one sense the just reaction to love squandered for so long. It is now part of the cycle of lies. True love can no longer be seen as it should be—as a home, as the inkling of heaven. Mary keeps seeking a place of consolation, of forgiveness and transformation. From the beginning to the end of this quiet tragedy, the need for *home* defines everything. Mary senses that a true and loving home is heaven:

> Never mind. The summer will soon be over, thank goodness. Your season will open again and we can go back to second-rate hotels and trains. I hate them, too, but at least I don't expect them to be like a home.... It never has been and it never will be [a home]....
> In a real home one is never lonely.
> —Eugene O'Neill, *Long Day's Journey into Night*

In the conscience of failed loves, it seems that the truth does not will out. What happens in such a sad situation where it seems there is no exit, no entrance for truth and love? The Tyrones have gone far down a road of masks formed by lies under the guide of protective love. They traded away truth for shades of truth. Then actual truth and love, having little or nowhere to go, were suppressed repeatedly until they appear as the opposite of themselves. If they continue to live by lies, they begin to die. But they will have a pleasant union, punctuated by the truth manifesting as resentment. If they try to remove the masks and live by love, their existential and deadly realizations will be fierce. It will overwhelm them with the power of hell. What is up will be down and what is down will be up, each as blind as someone who never had sight.

We have finished the tragedy of the conscience of failed love and the lost heaven it presents. The Tyrones need to tear off their masks for love to grow and not to be squandered. But their masks must remain for them to survive. The Tyrones could not bear the truth for they *have rendered the truth unbearable*! The family has done the impossible and made survival opposed to love. But love is the only thing that endures. Each family member has entered such a person-dissolving territory. What remains of their personhood is bound up in the other who is also dissolving. But among them they have enough substance to persist together. For one to risk tearing off the mask would be existential death, creating a domino effect of spiritual shock and demise in the others. It would quicken the protracted death that for now keeps them this side of life. They are ghosts of memory and regret and familial bond and even love, yes love. Eugene O'Neill sought to create a tragedy where persons could no longer call their souls their own, where "everything comes between you and what you'd like to be, and you've lost your true self forever." Here, love is so out of place that it seems it cannot be found again. Is this not the very risk of hell itself?

> It seemed to me that I could feel the Passion of Christ strongly, but yet I longed by God's grace to feel it more intensely. I thought how I wished I had been there at the crucifixion with Mary Magdalene and with others who were Christ's dear friends, that I might have seen in the flesh the Passion of our Lord which he suffered for me, so that I could have suffered with him as others did who loved him. . . . I wanted to suffer with him, while living in my mortal body, as God would give me grace. And suddenly I saw the red blood trickling down from under the crown of thorns.
> —St. Julian of Norwich, *Revelations of Divine Love*

12

What Can We Say about the Experience/Non-Experience of Death?

Lost Time, by Carol Scott

The Experience/Non-Experience of Death

I lay at the base of your back
You crack me open
Unbroken
All the fireflies
Of every world
Here around us
My breasts upon your back
Your affinity soft and firm
Floating into ether
Rising candles in infinite paper lanterns
I know this is to be my soul
I know that it could find you anywhere
You are constellation
The God knowing
The God trusting
The God praying
God's hands all over you
You are constellation

   —"You are Constellation," by Carol Scott & Caitlin Smith Gilson

> If ever immortality is conferred upon us, not just the soul but the entire physical human being will in some inconceivable manner participate in the life of the gods.... For what is in truth meant by this indestructability [of the soul] is the immortality, exceeding all conception—not of the soul, but of the whole man.
> —Josef Pieper, *Death and Immortality*

THE DEATH OF THE beloved presents us with the one experience we cannot understand or process as we do all other earthly experiences. How does the "I" complete the task of knowing, especially when confronted with the non-experience of death *as death*? The living—and even the dying—do not experience death *as it is*. Yet death invades all life, it defines and distinguishes all human experiences. We are haunted by our inability to know death. We cannot conceive of this radical pole to life, but it defines all experience. We feel death in the ending day, the setting sun, the days running out, the job we leave, the broken relationship, the graduation, the change of life. Every experience of change is a reminder of death within life.

We need to grasp this long shadow. We know that death is our lifelong companion and the most defining experience of human existence. This repeated inability to process death, realized in grief, must be given its proper place. We must dwell on death a little more before we can proceed faithfully into the question of the afterlife. Our experiences in the world are guideposts and in a way present in the afterlife because grace *perfects* nature and does not destroy it. The experience of death, which is most fundamental to us, especially realized in Christ's passion, cannot be neglected.

The death of the loved one, with all its grief and sorrow, is also a stumbling non-experience. Grief is uniquely the experience of non-experience. We cannot go that next step with the beloved, we do not undergo that next step and cannot understand *where* they are, even *what* they are. Our sorrow lengthens due to this non-experience inside the experience of grief. The inability to take in the beloved is a shocking loss! We have for so long interiorized the loved one in our thoughts and exteriorized ourselves to them. Our personhood is bound up in loving them. Their loss leaves a vacuum of experience, a painful wound inside our beings. How are we to go on? The loved one has also taken us in repeatedly and exteriorized ourselves for us, and now this beloved has died. What becomes of the other when she dies, and what becomes of us? Haven't the dead, through a lifelong process of interiorization and exteriorization, taken something of us with them to the grave? And yet we cannot quite experience death as we live and breathe.

The Experience/Non-Experience of Death

This is the mystery of death, which takes us in as we live and enter communion with others. Death smuggles us away when we die. In death, we take with us so much of our loved ones. In the rupture of the human essence, in that violent separation of body and soul, we also take that unity where personhood grows. Still death eludes all capture.

The experience of grief as the non-experience of death permeates our lives. Here, the widow recalls the beauty of the plumtree blossoms in her yard. They furiously bloom and call into presence her absent, dead husband and their years together. We can imagine when they were young, the two of them planting those trees happily with much life ahead of them:

> Sorrow is my own yard where the new grass flames as it has flamed often before but not with the cold fire that closes round me this year. Thirty-five years I lived with my husband.
> —William Carlos Williams, "The Widow's Lament in Springtime"

The widow cannot take in those flowers in the same way she did prior to his death. The blossoms are their shared life, the symbol of their future. Because of his death, the flowers remind her of what she has lost: both him and the self she was *with* him. The flowers are now unbearable, they are no longer what they were. Like the consecrated Host, only the outward eucharistic species is unchanged. The whole experience of the blossoms for the grieving widow is existentially altered. God is acting in the Eucharist, effecting a change in the inner reality of the elements. Death, in a mirrored way, affects the inner elements of our human experience. Outwardly, the world looks the same. But within the twofold process of interiorization of the beloved, and exteriorization of the self, the world has also become a foreign place. The salt loses its savor. The beauty of the blossoms can no longer be appreciated *as they were*. They are tinged with the non-experience of his death inside the experience of grief. The blossoms remind us of the tragic wisdom within our bodies and souls. The widow desires union again, she seeks to recover the flowers as they were, the experience as it was. She learns of other flowers growing at the edge of the heavy woods, down in the meadow, all white blossoms sinking into the marsh. She seeks out that experience as if to sink into it, to become inseparable from them. Perhaps only then will she know the dearest beloved again. This knowledge is what death cannot provide, but only death can facilitate its foreshadowing in our hope for heaven and for the resurrection of our bodies.

> The plumtree is white today with masses of flowers. Masses of flowers load the cherry branches and color some bushes yellow and some red but the grief in my heart is stronger than they for though they were my joy formerly, today I notice them and turn away forgetting. Today my son told me that in the meadows, at the edge of the heavy woods in the distance, he saw trees of white flowers. I feel that I would like to go there and fall into those flowers and sink into the marsh near them.
> —William Carlos Williams, *The Widow's Lament in Springtime*

In the normal course of knowledge, we put ourselves completely alongside the event, experiencing its many aspects and contours. But when we witness death, we are left at the precipice of meaning. We cannot take in what the dying loved one is experiencing, especially *after* death. We cannot understand the experience of *being* dead, for this takes on a state of non-experience. This is the knowledge we desire complete, not only because we wonder whether such finality is final but because it has *always* been present to us in our changing lives.

We see the child grow from infant to toddler, to young adult. All our experience has been shaped and refined by the little deaths that occur along the way in the growing of this life. There are so many little deaths that make up the moments, the hours, the days of our bodies, hearts, and minds. The last call, the last game, and all the firsts in existence that cannot help but extinguish something older that had put us closer to our immortality. Every change is growth and death. Every transcendence prepares us for dying. Every union necessitates parting, death cannot be contained. Death is wordless speech and unreceived listening. Death's touch caresses all as it holds nothing, and its caresses are inseparable from living and breathing. To consider it would be to grasp hold of something more intimate than our own selves.

> Consider the dying: do they not come at last to guess the hollowness of everything that we engage in here? Nothing is what it is! . . . To bear all death, the whole of death; death even before life; and gently, without rancor, to keep it, contain it, is terrible beyond all language.
> —Rainier Maria Rilke, *Duino Elegies*

We cannot take in the one experience, death, that provides the backdrop for everything we know about the world, others, and ourselves. This is shocking and profound. It signifies something important. We learn many things from knowledge. But we are also suspended from completely

The Experience/Non-Experience of Death

knowing ourselves. This non-experience of death has imprinted everything we know. When we know, we also experience the mystery that there is *more*, more we do not, indeed cannot, know while on earth. This uneasy mystery provides us with the hope for the afterlife, a hope coextensive with the deepest seat of our natures. Our knowledge shows us that we cannot know ourselves completely without what heaven gifts us. Most particularly, what the resurrection recovers from death. Every act of human knowledge attests to this powerful truth.

Let us approach once more our embodiment in relation to the Divine. God's creative action is not like our own. Our lives are a lifetime of protracted dying. When we create, there must always be this movement from the idea to reality, from the possible creation to the made creation, from an incomplete idea to a more complete knowledge. But God, who is pure reality, does not create in this way. His knowledge does not depend on things other than Himself for his action. He does not go from an incomplete idea to a more complete creation. Because God is perfect, all perfect knowledge and reality exist one with His Being. God's creation and reality are always present in Him, His Being. When he transfers this reality to His creatures, they participate in it by way of gaining and growing in knowledge particular to their natures. God has no potentiality. God is Reality Itself. Creatures have potentiality. They go from potentially full grown to full grown, potentially strong to strong, potentially knowledgeable to knowledgeable, and so on. Our potential for growth depends upon God's supreme Being, Who is always actual and the reality of all perfections and existence. This is why God's actuality *always* precedes our potentiality. God's reality enables us to participate in existence. When we move and act and engage of our own free will, we are participating in that original reality that God created for us. We are acting on the very *actuality* of God's Being. God is innermost in all things. This is an incredible indication of heaven as our permanent home. Our beings rise above the constraints of the material world and reveal themselves to be *knowing* participants in the reality God created for us. Indeed, we are *knowing* participants who sense God's infinite *actuality*, which alone can provide the foundation for finite creatures. God's existence precedes, exceeds, grounds, and unveils our reality.

> Now participated existence is limited by the capacity of the participator; so that God alone, Who is His own existence, is pure act and infinite.
> —St. Thomas Aquinas, *Summa Theologica* I, Question 75

We are not merely brains in a vat. If we were merely a series of synapses firing off in the brain, when flooded with sense impressions, we would forever be affected by external forces that alter, manipulate, change, and reduce us. We would not be persons. Personhood necessitates *a core stability* that allows us to *know* or recognize the non-experience of death inside grief. Our stable personhood knows that our creative action requires the God Who is all actual perfections so that we can ascend from possible knowledge to actual knowledge. The table exists but cannot in its own power preserve itself from being rotted, damaged, painted, or broken. This is certainly not analogous to a person. Our souls receive their stability through participating in God. God's *actual* existence is what our souls turn towards when knowing reality. This allows us to be able to see the forest for the trees. We are made in God's image and likeness. To be in God's image means we know the *Source* of our beings, we knowingly *participate* in that Source, and we *reflect* on that Source unlike any other creature. We interiorize and exteriorize that Source daily. In this respect, heaven is nearer to us than we realize!

Every natural thing has receptivity and activity. The ear is *actively* moved by the sound of the dog's barking. The dog is roused to bark when its eyes first *receive* sight of the cat scurrying across the lawn. Every natural thing reveals itself to be in this cause-and-effect cycle. There is always something else prior in that cycle. Natural causes possess a degree of "firstness." The cat must *first* scurry across the lawn, then the dog barks in response, and subsequently we hear the dog barking. In a similar way, the acorn is prior to the oak it subsequently causes. But both the acorn and the oak need something *else* to cause them. Every natural cause possesses potentiality or a dependency that recharacterizes what we mean by "first." Both the acorn and the tree needed something else to cause them. Before they existed, they had the potential to exist, but were dependent on something else to cause their existence. When they do exist, they have the potential to grow but need things other than themselves, such as the air, water, soil, and nutrients. When we look at natural causes, they reveal that none is *truly* first, each is a secondary or dependent cause. Every natural cause may cause or generate something else. It is prior to what it causes. But the acorn and the oak are in the same boat—they both need something other than themselves for their existence. All these natural causes are generated by something else. All "firsts" in nature are not *truly* first! This particular acorn is before this particular oak, but it is not truly first.

It needed something *else* for its existence. The true First must be existence itself, it must be *purely actual*, always existing, and innermost in all things. God is the true First that allows us to act on His creation that He gives us. When we reflect on the world, we see many things that appear to be first but are not truly first. Every natural cause depends upon something else for its existence, therefore, they are all *secondary* or *intermediary* causes. But you cannot have secondary or intermediary causes without a First Cause! Every natural cause in the world points to the Divine as its true First Cause. How astonishing that when we experience the world, we experience the natural desire for heaven. God is paradise.

Our intellects are receptive, receiving information from our senses. The very *experience* of that receptivity first involves action, which points us to God. I can receive sound through my ears only because I *actively* have the capacity to hear. There is an aspect of our souls understood to be purely active, containing no potentiality. This is what allows us to be in God's image. We are not merely passive beings reacting to sensations inside an environment. We have a core stable personhood transcending our environment. We can *actively* reach out into the world and *know* we are reaching out. We can *actively* seek out the sound we would like to hear, and *actively* seek out the food we would like to taste. We form our worlds. This aspect of us is closest to the essence of God and of God creating the world. Our capacity to learn, to actualize our desires, points to the Divine because it points to a transcendent foundation within us. We are not reducible to the material world, to our environment, or to our sensations; we are "world-forming."

> Bees navigate and forage by living out a range of relevance specified by the good of the hive. They notice sources of nectar, but they don't contemplate the intelligibility of the flower or the beauty of the bloom; there are no bee botanists or bee poets. Now, this might seem like a trivial point. After all, there are no human drones or human hives. But phenomenologists are not calling attention to random differences between bees and humans. They are highlighting the character of the fundamental difference that makes the observation of this difference possible. The bee or any other animal is inscribed within the domain of an environment. Humans, by contrast, can transcend their environment and dwell within the world. As a result, they can compare one environment with another.
> —Chad Engelland, *Phenomenology*

On earth, our human nature comes closest to reflecting God. We clearly see the cycle of life wholly binding the plant and animal to their environment. But we transcend our environment and can ask the questions *about* environments. I can actively choose to go to the lecture and place myself in a state of receptivity. I can choose to make fundamental connections. But we are body and soul. And our bodies, like that of every other creature, are bound to a lifecycle. This lifecycle and how our souls engage with our bodies makes each of us unique. We are each unrepeatable in our image and likeness to God. Our birth, growth, maturation, and death reflect St. Thomas's remarks that a longer way was assigned to man than to the angels for our happiness. We experience the image of God *through time*. Our souls experience eternal realities *through our bodies*. This is the powerhouse meaning of our bodies. They are not transient and only temporal, as the plant, but the moving image of the eternal. Our bodies are raised into the dignity of God's divine image, especially manifest in Christ.

In experience and knowledge, we repeatedly take in the beloved who has previously taken us in. This is the intensifying cycle of human life. When we know and love another human being through time and decades, we reveal inklings of the interconnectedness promised in our glorified bodies. In paradise, each person overflows in goodness and love into others as a fulfillment of our *always* shared existence, cut short by sin. Death reminds us that these inklings we experience of union with the beloved are at best traces, glimmers of what we hope is to come in heaven. We sense the glorified union all our lives, we sense it in love, but we cannot fulfill this union on earth, death cuts it terribly short. C. S. Lewis reflects on life after the death of his wife:

> At first, I was very afraid of going to places where H. and I had been happy—our favorite pub, our favorite wood. But I decided to do it at once—like a pilot up again as soon as possible after he's had a crash. Unexpectedly, it makes no difference. Her absence is no more emphatic in those places than anywhere else. It's not local at all. I suppose that if one were forbidden all salt one wouldn't notice it much more in any one food than in another. Eating in general would be different, every day, at every meal. It is like that. The act of living is different all through. Her absence is like the sky, spread over everything. But no, that is not quite accurate. There is one place where her absence comes locally home to me, and it is a place I can't avoid. I mean my own body. It had such a different

> importance while it was the body of H.'s lover. Now it's like an empty house.
> —C. S. Lewis, *A Grief Observed*

When we experience the death of the loved one, we experience the rupture of our beings. We know ourselves through relationship. We are perpetually interiorizing and exteriorizing our selves and the loved one. It is the process where we learn our own selves and the beloved. This process is held suspended; through death, it is refused completion. In grief, we feel this process being halted, we feel the incomplete ends, and through this we hope for heaven and the gift of resurrection. This fugitive essence, death, has been our companion in all human experience; it has defined, distinguished, and delineated all events. From our first acts of knowing to our last, we have repeatedly engaged death *because* it first engaged us. Every act of knowledge is a reminder that one must go through death to live. Death is the one experience, the one reality, we do not process, and it is inside *all* experiences. In all knowledge we feel incomplete and desire to know completely. We must press on even further. Every act of knowledge taunts us with that unknown presence of death. All acts of knowledge whisper into our ears: *you have not learned it all, you have had the experiences, again and again, but missed the meaning; until you understand death, until you know it, you have not completed knowledge, nor known yourself.* Earth cannot complete this knowledge and we are rational animals, *knowing* beings. It is our very nature to know. In knowledge we see time and again the hope for heaven as true completion. We live a life entwined in death, knowing there is something we cannot yet know. Only God's eternal life can grant this wisdom.

In grief we learn the deep desire for the glorified body. Death of the beloved places us in exile. When we mourn, we experience the beginnings of our *own* torn separation of body and soul. We have lost the beloved who shared us as we shared them. We are torn apart. In grief, we are on the hunt for the one home that can complete what is lacking on earth. The reality of dying stamps everything we know with a *penultimate* nature. Everything in life stops short of completion. Just as all natural causes can never be "first." All our lives we are never complete. Death stops us in our tracks. This is the birthplace of *desire*. We desire to transcend from the penultimate to the ultimate:

> O Lord God of hosts, convert us: and shew thy face, and we shall be saved.
> —Psalm 80:19

Christ has overcome death. This is a magnificent gift. Christ has given us eternal life and through Him we can take in what death once left unexperienced, once cut short. In paradise, we can complete that process of interiorization and exteriorization of the beloved which death destroyed. In the glorified state, Christ's body becomes for us the unseen made visible through the chorus of creatures in praise and joy. Each is united to His body and blood. Our blindness is transformed into sight. Our earthly loss is repossessed in Christ. Christ's flesh and blood communalizes all things in the glorified state. In grief, happiness, peace, and heartache, we turn to the world, unable to find a corresponding image reflecting those experiences. This recognition of our blindness, cornerstone of every honest human life, illustrates our longing for heaven. Only when we are united to Christ in the beatific vision will we have the proper image and source of all joy. Christ is the source that conquers death, the visible imprint of the eternal, which we have been looking for all our earthly lives.

Our personhood is simultaneously exteriorized within the world through our bodies and through community. We are interiorized through our image and likeness to God, Who is innermost in all His creatures. Due to our fallenness, death entered us and all our relationships. Death refuses to be understood, it overwhelms us. We cannot complete the understanding of death. Every act of our knowledge is grounded on the non-experience of death. All things learned remind us of the innermost and overarching source of knowledge near us but unable to be experienced. All acts of knowledge encourage us to seek greater completion. Everything groans for God Who alone can experience death and overcome it. All our knowledge seeks what Christ alone accomplishes. Heaven is not a tributary to existence but its estuary.

In knowledge, we desire reality. We seek to know the object or idea in question in its fullness. But we *never* complete an understanding of the things of the world. Everything in the world is coextensive with the experience of death. Every existing thing undergoes decay, disease, and death. Knowledge is a humbling experience. We learn much but we also learn that we do *not* know. Death cannot be taken in; it cannot be experienced as other things are experienced. Every act of knowledge reveals our failure to know completely. This failure can only be overturned in heaven. Our desire for heaven is not a peripheral wish to life but its central defining reality. We are not Christ; we cannot overcome death. Because of our image and likeness to God, we stand on the horizon between time and eternity for we are bodies and intellectual souls. We are *knowers* held suspended from innermost reality. We *knowingly* groan inwardly for God, knowing something is missing in our experience of knowledge. We know that the earth in its bondage to death and decay cannot provide us full knowledge. We are always missing the crucial piece of the puzzle. We know we have had the experiences, all our lives, but missed the meaning, and we are seeking that Home that restores the experience in a different form altogether:

> For the creation waits with eager longing for the revealing of the children of God; for the creation was subjected to futility, not of its own will but by the will of the one who subjected it, in hope that the creation itself will be set free from its bondage to decay and will obtain the freedom of the glory of the children of God. We know that the whole creation has been groaning in labor pains until now; and not only the creation, but we ourselves, who have the first fruits of the Spirit, groan inwardly while we wait for adoption, the redemption of our bodies.
> —Romans 8:19–23

Christ turns the tables upside down. In the Gospel of John, He turned to Martha and said: *"I am the Resurrection and the life. Those who believe in me, even though they die, will live, and everyone who lives and believes in me will never die."* In Christ, death *can* be taken in. Through His sacrifice, we have the power to take in this force that is the long shadow defining every life and had once defeated us. Christ has placed sin and death into His very being, He has tasted death for all, paid its once insurmountable wages, and overturned death, overcoming the world. With St. Ambrose we can say that Christ has made "heaven a house of bread." Our Savior has revealed death as no longer the end and now as the way *through* to knowledge and salvation. In our relationship with Christ, we can interiorize and exteriorize ourselves and the beloved. Through Him, what is truly lost is found again and, in a way, completely new. Christ offers His body and blood at the Last Supper knowing that death awaited Him. He experienced total abandonment, the terrible powers of death. All knowledge collapsed, all interiorization and exteriorization unraveled. Only God can put the pieces back together. Christ knew that the way to salvation was not through a sidestepping of the consequences of human action but *through* death. He made death, once the enemy of life and knowledge, the way to heaven and eternal wisdom.

> Every soul which receives the bread which comes down from Heaven is a house of bread, the bread of Christ, being nourished and having its heart strengthened by the support of the heavenly

> bread which dwells within it. Hence Paul says: "We are all one bread."
> —St. Ambrose, *Letters* XI

Transubstantiation is the supreme offer of life. It mirrors, even as it overturns, the power of death. Death is the unwieldy tool Christ had to work with in completing the mission of salvation. It is through death that He unfastens the nails from the cross and chisels away at the stone across the tomb. Christ used His own death to overcome death for all persons. The eucharistic species remains unchanged—we see the razed wheat, the temporality, the finitude. The thin shell of a wafer reflects the experience *as* non-experience of death. Inwardly, the experience of the Eucharist is the superabundance of life. When we consume the Eucharist, we have experienced death overcome.

> The Christian religion is the only one that, overlooking the supremely evident fact of the mortality of the flesh—which has pushed all other religions towards spiritualization as the only possible path to Salvation—has found in the flesh, in the mortal, eucharistic, mystical, resurrecting flesh, the unsurpassable end of the ways of God. This concrete, extremely problematic man who is imprisoned and sunk in his flesh: God has him and no other in view; he intends to become one, truly "one flesh," with him.
> —Hans Urs von Balthasar, *Theo-Logic II*

The Son was pinned to the dead tree of failed ends. He not only aged through all the ages, with skin broken, faded, and parched, bones quaking beneath, but did so as the joy within the womb. While dying, He was also the child nourished on the breast. Christ is always near His mother's heart, a holy innocent ever cradled in her embrace. His thirst in dying is His thirst in the manger. From cradle to cross, Christ enters our lives to overcome death and return us to living. My God, my God, this is the exquisite gift made by Your surrender, by You being forsaken. The child is simultaneously the crucified Lord and will bear what we cannot. Christ gives up the only ghost worthy to inhabit flesh and blood. Unless we be like this child, we cannot enter the kingdom of heaven. Please make us ready for hope.

> We can only speak of creation as having been brought into being by and for its savior Jesus Christ, and its whole history as having been providentially [shaped] by him, from the moment that he is revealed within its history, as the Passion. Theologically speaking, creation and its history begins with the Passion of Christ and from this "once for all" work looks backwards and forwards to see

The Experience/Non-Experience of Death

> everything in this light, making everything new. Christian cosmology, elaborated as it must be from the perspective of the Cross, sees the Cross as impregnated in the very structure of creation: *stat crux dum volvitur orbis*—the Cross stands, while the earth revolves.
> —John Behr, *The Mystery of Christ: Life in Death*

We seek also to glimpse the restlessness so deeply reflected in the teachings on purgatory, as sweet suffering antechamber to heaven. While disappointing, it is not surprising that prayers for souls in purgatory have diminished. It is an unmistakable symptom of the loss of heaven. When we lose heaven, our permanent home, we emaciate the transcendent figure at root which realizes human nature. When we lose purgatory, we lose our arduous mystical hope, and replacing it with empty wish-fulfillment or nihilistic despair. When we lose the threat of hell, by either encamping in the prideful certainty of its existence (more often for others) or equally false certainty of its irrelevance or non-existence, we become reflections of a diminished love that has now traded itself for lies dressed up *as love*. These are the lies that caress only to deform human nature, society, politics, and human relations. The union of body and soul has always been the key to sustaining a glimpse of paradisal perfection. Only through it can we then encounter the mystery of death as passageway to what it is to be persons, through Christ, co-creating the very architecture of heaven.

> You never enjoy the world aright, till the Sea itself floweth in your veins, till you are clothed with the heavens, and crowned with the stars: and perceive yourself to be the sole heir of the whole world, and more than so, because men are in it who are every one sole heirs as well as you. Till you can sing and rejoice and delight in God, as misers do in gold, and Kings in sceptres, you never enjoy the world. Till your spirit filleth the whole world, and the stars are your jewels; till you are as familiar with the ways of God in all Ages as with your walk and table: till you are intimately acquainted with that shady nothing out of which the world was made: till you love men so as to desire their happiness, with a thirst equal to the zeal of your own: till you delight in God for being good to all: you never enjoy the world. Till you more feel it than your private estate, and are more present in the hemisphere, considering the glories and the beauties there than in your own house: till you remember how lately you were made, and how wonderful it was when you came into it: and more rejoice in the palace of your glory, than if it had been made but to-day morning.
> —Thomas Traherne, *Centuries of Meditations*

PART II

What Is the Resurrected State Like?

Spirit of Our Lady of Holy Cross, by Carol Scott

On the train, transported back-and-forth daily, nonstop, relentless
  movement,
Tired into the spirit fatigue, I am certain that if you looked at me
The way you do, my eyes are not as bright, the shadow music of the train's
  whistle
I close my eyes, only to get a break, to enter something other nothing
It is there that I can feel my lover, the one I love, your kiss, the weight of it
So light I think it is a strand of my own hair falling on my lips
Between waking and sleep, even this and I am alive again
The long opened door, the sound of it separating and rejoining
It closes and another stop is passed, your near absence hovering
The shunting sigh of the brakes released, I can barely skate this surface
To give you, the gravitational pull of this train, bonded to metal track
A vortex lingers between distances, something in me happened
Layers and volleys and images, a structural world reached, into the orbit
And made me a body in motion, you have entered me in ways I cannot
  grasp
In sleep those strands on my lips, haunted line of boxed steel cars waking
Layering volleying imagistic play with the silhouette in the windows of the
  train
Say any words any at all and the Song of Songs, something other
You are the opened door of another stop, you have pierced through
My whole center with a sword, in some way you extinguished me
So gentle I barely know that I am transfixed, affixed to every passing
  scenery
Out these windows till I am back to you, no one can undress me as you do
I barely know enough, this torrent, these strands on my lips, I thought it
  was you
My heavy eyes flowing through the train

—"On the Train," by Caitlin Smith Gilson

The most hardened warrior has been a tender infant nourished with milk; and the toughest martyr, the strongest martyr tortured on the iron horse, the martyr with the roughest bark, the most wrinkled skin, the strongest martyr on the rack and in the thumbscrew has been a tender, milky child.
—Charles Péguy, *The Mystery of the Holy Innocents*

13

Our Five Senses

Signposts of the Resurrected State and Our Fallenness

Light Sauce, by Carol Scott

What is the quiet exactly that we need for sleep, that we need?
I can still hear the singer's voice rising and falling, foreign and close
Italian poetry, the room turned into trees, infinite trees, someday burning inside us
How much more of life do we give, do we receive, how much more I do not know
A life died today, I do not know, I will not know, rising and falling eternity
Random life filled with heartbreaking randomness, these entwined patterns
Too intricate to see, random to you and to me, to give and to receive
I could die tomorrow, I could fail to wake, it is really living to know this dying
To know things passing, this flesh, my body ages, it wants what it wants
To be kissed, covered again, to hear you rising and falling
Infinite tree, infinite memory, burning
What is the quiet exactly that we need for sleep, that we need? Is it absence of noise?
All I know is that I need you asleep next to me, that is the quiet, that is the need
Given and received, burning up in me, quiet speaks volumes, I hear the silence
Loud in my heart, beating, pumping, sound of your touch
Ear listening to the space between voices, the wordless said, I know you
You don't need to speak, I hear your song, at this very moment
I am walking the path to the water again, I doubt I see a soul between the dunes
Rising and falling, everyone congregating, the caffe in sun, Sunday drawn
The Basilica soon to sound its bells, family life
Somewhere the sound of your touch hides, swells of the sea
Is this the absence of noise? How much more of life do we give, do we receive?
How much more I do not know

—"The Wordless Said," by Carol Scott & Caitlin Smith Gilson

To engage such questions as friendship, play, whether our animals accompany us in the resurrected state, the status of spousal unions and intimate relationships, we must first reflect on the nature of the glorified body. This is essential for any meaningful glimpse of paradise. Our glorified bodies exceed and elevate the very best and most virtuous dispositions of our earthly bodies. But glorification works from within grace, perfecting nature, not destroying it. Our attention must return to the lifelong elegy of the senses. We must return to what it means to be flesh and blood. And we look once more to *why* we are beings on the horizon between time and eternity. This is our immortality.

Our earthly senses are always placing us outside of ourselves and within the manifold experiences of the world. The body's very architecture is to yearn, unite, and extend in and towards world, nature, people, animals, and beauty. Let us pay serious attention to the scriptural expressions of our senses. Our sense experiences do reflect a spiritual life. In the lowly senses dwells the hope for the resurrection of our bodies. They are often overlooked as one of the ways we are in the image and likeness of God. Through our senses, we unearth manifold layers of intensifying relationships. Our sense experience is a kaleidoscopic richness that prefigures the incarnational power of Word made flesh and blood. Our soul is not meant to be abstract or disembodied but to have shape, breadth, length, texture, sound, and fragrance. Our soul united to our bodies is meant to enliven the ecstatic reaches of human beings who live on the horizon between time and eternity.

We will avoid the anemic spiritualism that forsakes the senses. Our senses are not something shed along the way to enlightenment. Nor is sense experience something that reduces us to mere animals. Our senses enable us to experience life in a uniquely *human* and incarnational way.

Smell

> So he went to him and kissed him. When Isaac caught the smell of his clothes, he blessed him and said, "Ah, the smell of my son is like the smell of a field that the LORD has blessed. May God give you heaven's dew and earth's richness—an abundance of grain and new wine."
> —Genesis 27:27–28

> An odor of a sweet smell, a sacrifice acceptable, well pleasing to God.
> —Philippians 4:18

> Instead of fragrance there will be a stench; instead of a sash, a rope; instead of well-dressed hair, baldness; instead of fine clothing, sackcloth; instead of beauty, branding. I hate, I despise your religious festivals; your assemblies are a stench to me. Even though you bring me burnt offerings and grain offerings, I will not accept them. Though you bring choice fellowship offerings, I will have no regard for them.
> —Amos 5:21–22

> A third of the human race was killed by these three plagues—by the fire, the smoke, and the sulfur that came from their mouths.
> —Revelation 9:18

In the sacrifice of the Mass, the incense billows into the air, wafting between the material and the immaterial. The smoke is the visible presence of our prayers commingling with the Word of God, uniting heaven and earth. As the Psalmist wrote: *"Let my prayer rise like incense before you. The lifting of my hands like the evening offering."* In the nativity of our Lord, myrrh and frankincense are gifts given by the magi, which foreshadow Christ as the only person born to die. Fragrance permeates his swaddling clothes, the winding funeral linen, and the tomb. Mary Magdalene took a pound of precious scented ointment and anointed the feet of Jesus. She wiped his feet with her hair: and the whole house was perfumed with the fragrance. In all this goodness, we know Judas's betrayal is another scent wafting in the room. He asks why the ointment wasn't sold and given to the poor? Jesus replies that the poor you will always have, but Me not always.

This redolence attached itself to Christ throughout His life. It enshrines prayer and rises forth in the Book of Revelation to reveal what is veiled, within the presence of judgment itself. The angel in Revelation comes and stands by the altar with a gold censer and heaps of incense to offer up with prayers before the throne. *"The smoke of the incense along with the prayers of the holy ones went up before God from the hand of the angel."* Scent is also present in the Scriptures as the antithesis to the perfume of sanctity. Instead, we are accosted with the noxious waste in which sin damages human relationships. This smell is aligned with the stench of decomposition and death. In Deuteronomy, we hear of burning soil, the smell of sulfur, all is a wasteland, and nothing can grow. It becomes almost impossible to avoid inhaling that death. We have traded the breath of life for something else altogether. We can imagine the smells on Golgotha. Christ beaten, bruised for all the sins unto death. All the stench and decay Christ must have taken into His Being:

> Dislocated, almost ripped out of their sockets, the arms of the Christ seemed trammelled by the knotty cords of the straining muscles. The laboured tendons of the armpits seemed ready to snap. The fingers, wide apart, were contorted in an arrested gesture in which were supplication and reproach but also benediction. The trembling thighs were greasy with sweat. The ribs were like staves, or like the bars of a cage, the flesh swollen, blue, mottled with flea-bites, specked as with pin-pricks by spines broken off from the rods of the scourging and now festering beneath the skin where they had penetrated. Purulence was at hand. The fluvial wound in the side dripped thickly, inundating the thigh with blood that was like congealing mulberry juice, . . . the knees had been forced together, twisting the shins outwardly over the feet which stapled one on top of the other, had begun to putrefy and turn green beneath the seeping blood. . . . Above this eruptive cadaver, the head, tumultuous, enormous, encircled by a disordered crown of thorns, hung down lifeless. One lacklustre eye half opened as a shudder of terror or of sorrow traversed the expiring figure. . . . The torture had been unendurable, and the agony had frightened the mocking executioners into flight.
> —J. K. Huysmans, *The Damned*

But Christ had also been a child, "a tender milky child." He is always for us both the nativity and the passion. And the perfume of each is within each of us. We carry the sweet scent of life and the terrible scent of death as impossible but truly given promise of life. The mother takes the newborn child in her arms and closes her eyes. She places her face, buries her nose into the crown of the child's head. She breathes in the sweetness of the holy innocent who smells of manna, honey, and of spirit. Every mother at that moment is a Marian figure, breathing in Our Lady and Our Lord:

> Their new souls, their fresh souls.
> Fresh in the morning, fresh at noon, fresh in the evening.
> Fresh like the roses of France.
> —Charles Péguy, *The Portal of the Mystery of Hope*

In scent and smell we come to a primal experience that most immediately responds to God's breath of life. Our in-spiration/inhalation of the child's new life corresponds to Our Lord's expiration/exhalation of His spirit in the forming of the world: *"And the* Lord *God formed man of the dust of the ground, and breathed into his nostrils the breath of life; and man became a living soul."* And it is there in the haunting, lingering perfume of grief where clothes are pulled into one's arms and smelled, taken deeply into the lungs, placing presence within the absence. In this valley of dry and deadened bones, our inhalation, even in all its shallow breaths punctuated by weeping, is synonymous with hope. *"O dry bones, hear the word of the* Lord, *. . . I will cause breath to enter you that you may come to life."* The scent of the transcendence of the beloved, our breath that takes in the beloved, acts out the longer way of our spiritual embodiment. In breathing, our bodies physically yearn for the resurrection. We are relentlessly seeking the breath that not only prolongs life but returns us to eternality. The desire for the glorified state is not a mere sociological idea put on for this time or that. It is rhythmically present in every human being, in every inhalation and exhalation of the spirit. It is as foundational as our sense of smell. The desire for eternal life is in the taking in of the world through the air. It is in the fragrance brought into the center of our beings, to be commingled with our own vital essence and exhaled in image and likeness of the divine breath.

Touch

> And he arose and came to his father. But while he was still a long way off, his father saw him and felt compassion, and ran and embraced him and kissed him.
> —Luke 15:20

> Then he poured water into a basin and began to wash the disciples' feet and to wipe them with the towel that was wrapped around him.
> —John 13:15

> Then the Lord put out his hand and touched my mouth. And the Lord said to me, "Behold, I have put my words in your mouth."
> —Jeremiah 1:9

> And taking him aside from the crowd privately, he put his fingers into his ears, and after spitting touched his tongue.
> —Mark 7:33

> But God said, "You shall not eat of the fruit of the tree that is in the midst of the garden, neither shall you touch it, lest you die."
> —Genesis 3:3

> And if anyone touches an unclean thing, whether human uncleanness or an unclean beast or any unclean detestable creature, and then eats some flesh from the sacrifice of the LORD's peace offerings, that person shall be cut off from his people.
> —Leviticus 7:21

Touch is the fundamental sense that reflects our intimate union with the uncreated. God, the uncreated, touches the finger of Adam and we are. The Creator is eternal, and His touch never leaves us. This means that we have an intense immediacy of union with the uncreated God Who enables existence. This touch precedes all. All the other five senses in dialogue with God and the world have a difference, a separation. But in touch, God is an immediate and binding unity with us. Each sense carries within it greater and varying degrees of distance. Most noticeably is sight, which is an achievement over a length or space. But touch reminds us of this irreducibility, of this sheerness of power and presence that precedes everything in us. God's immediate and binding touch grounds all our reflection and knowledge. We become in touch as close as physically possible to becoming identical with the object. The object is tactically held and consumed by hands, pressed directly against our lips and cheeks. The tangible features of an object's warmth, texture, size, shape, and weight are experienced in an immediacy of union.

When ourselves and others are no longer objects but the lover and beloved, touch carries with it the greatest and painful hope, the tragic sense that we can raise the dead. We innately feel that the most consuming, passionate, and intimate touch, the touch with the most ecstatic love, could cross the divide. We sense that our touch could dive through the flesh into the uncreated God, Who always touches us, and recover our lost immortality. But no matter how much love and gentleness abound, we each enact the hereditary kiss of Judas on Christ. We furiously seek the everlasting bond but instead hand goodness, along with ourselves, over to death.

"Jesus asked him, 'Judas, are you betraying the Son of Man with a kiss?'" Touch places us squarely within the humbling reality that we cannot complete transcendence. We cannot recover what is lost. We are pressing our fingers to a mirror image of what is lost. We can feel its contours gnawing at our fingertips. In the embrace of the prodigal son, touch offers only a temporary union. It claims only a transient spiritual enjoining. We hold and hold the beloved longer than time allows. But this embrace must end. Each of us is parted by death. Touch, most particularly in marriage vows, is the

audacious and central promise that we can overcome the kiss of betrayal and become truly one. *"They are no longer two but one flesh. What therefore God has joined together, let no one separate."* How dearly we hope that we can grasp the glory that left us long ago. Only a sense of it remains in our touch, which caresses everything but holds on to nothing. In touching the beloved, we seek salvation that can hold on through every age, through time, memory, recollection, and forgetfulness. Every act of touch is a reminder of paradise and of our failure to complete the task, to find our way back to our permanent Home.

> If only I may touch His clothes, I shall be made well.
> —Mark 5:28

Hearing

> To him the gatekeeper opens. The sheep hear his voice, and he calls his own sheep by name and leads them out. When he has brought out all his own, he goes before them, and the sheep follow him, for they know his voice.
> —John 10:3–4

> Behold, I stand at the door and knock. If anyone hears my voice and opens the door, I will come into him and eat with him, and he with me.
> —Revelation 3:20

> And they heard the sound of the LORD God walking in the garden in the cool of the day, and the man and his wife hid themselves from the presence of the LORD God among the trees of the garden.
> —Genesis 3:8

> We know that God does not listen to sinners, but if anyone is a worshiper of God and does his will, God listens to him.
> —John 9:31

"In the beginning was the Word, and the Word was with God, and the Word was God. The same was in the beginning with God." Our existence, life, meaning, the root of all action begin in responsiveness. Our lives first begin in a listening to the Word which brings us into life itself, as in the image of the Word. *"God said, 'Let us make man in our image, after our likeness.'"* Our lives are the reception of God into our hearts and minds. This is most originally experienced in hearing, the original foundation for interiorizing and exteriorizing the beloved. Our existence responds to the Word. Our

lives necessitate listening to the divine call, which blesses and gives our unique human nature. In Genesis 1 God creates existence, dividing the dark from the light, the waters above from the waters below, the sea from the land, filling the oceans, sky, and earth with living beings. We learn that the creation of these glorious things is leading to a radical form of image and likeness. These creations evoke "it was so" and "it is good." But as God turns to created human beings in His image and likeness, He initiates the call and response of our relationship. The call and response as foundational to our lives on earth as signpost of heaven. The beginning of our existence is hearing God's word as blessing:

> God blessed them and said to them, "Be fruitful and increase in number; fill the earth and subdue it. Rule over the fish in the sea and the birds in the sky and over every living creature that moves on the ground."
> —Genesis 1:28

We are created in this divine call. But our natures, in the *image* of the Word, are fulfilled only when we hear and obey that call. We are created to hear and respond to God's call. This raises us above all other creatures. Our excellence is that God made us in His own image by giving us an intellectual soul. The intellectual soul realizes itself by responding to God's word. This act raises us above the beasts of the field that are only in God's likeness. We have the general likeness that pertains to all created things. This is the *unknowing* and good result of being created by God. But because human beings are freed to hear God's call, our likeness also has another sense, a likening power. We knowingly act in ways that enact a deeper correlation to the image of God. This unique likening power is seen in the cultivation of virtues through the union of human and divine love. A cultivation dependent upon hearing the word intrinsic to our beings. For Aquinas, this likening power even places us *relatively* higher than the angels. We have the opportunity over our lifetime to engage that hearing of God's call. Listening is the central act that helps us interiorize and exteriorize ourselves and others, particularly the beloved. Listening grounds how we become united to others, how the soul in a way becomes all things in knowledge. While the image of God is far more perfect in the angel than human beings, due to their intellectual powers, we have a dignity, a likening power, within the *entirety* of our flesh that can raise us above the angels.

We were made to hear the Word Who *"was made flesh, and dwelt among us (and we beheld his glory, the glory as of the only begotten of the*

Father), full of grace and truth." Hearing is not a mere collating of random unrelated sounds. When we hear we are obeying the reality of creation, and more interiorly, the Word. *If* there are things, there is a *way* for things to be. Only if there is a *way* for things to be is there meaning. Otherwise, one has at best indecipherable noise. In hearing, our senses are triggered beyond themselves through the act of relationship with creation, which shares with us the way things are. This is why a foreign language at first sounds too quick, run together, indistinct. This remains the case until the sound hides! Then the event of reality, the pattern, action, and meaning come to the forefront through gained understanding. Just as in learning a new language, all genuine hearing intrinsically involves a turning of one's whole being to the words. Hearing is an *obedience* to assimilating oneself to the reality of creation, which enables one to know oneself and others. Only when the foreign language ceases to be heard as sound and finally is heard as meaning, do we arrive at the depth of hearing as obedience. In hearing, we obediently turn our whole being to the other thing or person, to take in what is offered by that other.

> Note that if I think of what I am going to say, the word already exists in my heart. But if I want to speak to you, I am concerned to render present to your heart what is already present in mine. Then, seeking a way to let the word that exists in me reach you and dwell with you, I have recourse to my voice. Its sound communicates my word, and its meaning to you. When it is finished it vanishes. But my word is now in you, without ever having left me. I ask you God, to reveal me to myself.
> —St. Augustine, *The Confessions*

In God's divine call, our hearing is completed through obedience. True hearing is identical with obedience to the truth. Through the complete reception of the other, our souls become, in a way, all things. The sound communicates the Word that dwells in us. The sound fades, but the reception remains. We receive so that we may act. We are obedient so we may be free. We hear so that Christ will make his home in us. Through obedience, Christ makes His home in us:

> Anyone who loves me will obey my teaching. My Father will love them, and we will come to them and make our home with them. Anyone who does not love me will not obey my teaching. These words you hear are not my own; they belong to the Father who sent me.
> —John 14:23-24

Our original hearing of God's word *as* blessing evokes obedience to the ground of truth. This enables that separation of noise from meaning, the unreal from reality, untruth from truth. Noise is the foreign and unable to be received anti-language. It is looking through a glass darkly. But our hearing, one with obedience, was designated by God's call to uncover truth. The Word made flesh beckoned us at the moment of our creation to hear and to take in meaning, truth, goodness, beauty, and action.

In hearing, we experience heaven on earth because we have heard and taken in the call of creation as word and blessing. Through this original listening, we become in a way all things. This obedience to the word permeates within us our yearning for paradise. That first hearing of God's word fills us with the eternal presence of the divine. Our excellence consists in the dramatic gift of hearing and responding to our image and likeness. This indelibly reveals our end as only realized in heaven, most particularly in the resurrected state. The hope for the resurrection of the bodies is justified within the senses, especially within hearing as first enactment of our capacity for relationship. The glorified body properly reflects and fulfills the dignity of the senses. Our hearing, when truly attuned, becomes a co-creator in the architecture of heaven. Remember, our likening power relatively raises us in our embodiment above the angels!

Sight

> Now the appearance of the glory of the LORD was like a devouring fire on the top of the mountain in the sight of the people of Israel.
> —Exodus 24:17

> Again, Jesus spoke to them, saying, "I am the light of the world. Whoever follows me will not walk in darkness but will have the light of life."
> —John 8:12

> The LORD will smite you with madness and with blindness and with bewilderment of heart.
> —Deuteronomy 28:28

> And why do you see the speck that is in your brother's eye, but do not notice the beam of wood in your own eye?
> —Matthew 7:3

> Let them alone: they are blind, and leaders of the blind. And if the blind lead the blind, both will fall into the pit.
> —Matthew 15:14

Our Five Senses

Sight is the privileged sense that gives us access into our *longer way*, the journey of our lives. It gives us vision of the relationship of our flesh and spirit. In sight, we can see the forest for the trees. Sight enables us to understand our distance, our own distinction, the difference between ourselves and the other creatures that also participate in the world. There are times when our hands in their immediacy cannot touch. And smell in its inspiration cannot yet inhale the far-off fragrance. And hearing cannot yet receive. But sight alone can gaze upon that difference that the soul has not yet taken in. Sight renders us historical beings. Vision stretches us into the presence of experiences, beings, objects, artifacts which necessitate a story, an order, a cause-and-effect relationship. All these things can soon be taken in by our intellects in their interplay of meanings. Sight first glimpses them. Every experience of sight stretches us back into memory and meaning. One enters an antique shop and scans the room, taking in generational layers of existence. The dented guitar, a porcelain figurine, a tea set from India, the travel case from another century, a Madonna with its paint chipped. Each object enables us to envision their interrelatedness in time and history. In sight, we connect the world of things. Our vision helps us uncover aspects of an invisible string from one to another, forming a netting of unity. We unveil that unity and connectivity when we see these objects in their place. This is only heightened when we see another person who also sees us, whose sight is also one long, ever-connected engagement stretching from eternity into time.

> In the household where a new child is born, all objects change their sense, they begin to anticipate from this child some still indeterminate treatment, someone new and someone additional is there, a new history, whether it be brief or long, has just been established, and a new register is open. My first perception, along with the horizons that surround it, is an ever-present event, an unforgettable tradition; even as a thinking subject I am still this first perception, I am the continuation of the same life that it inaugurated.
> —Maurice Merleau-Ponty, *Phenomenology of Perception*

Time and space are given within sight. In seeing other things and people, we experience ourselves as the center or nucleus. We engage other beings and things which contain, protracted within them, the past and future. Things are held at a distance, even as they are brought forward for closer inspection. We experience in sight of something other the uniqueness of ourselves. The past and future are unveiled within the sight of the other.

Time dilates alongside our own recollections and anticipations. In sight, we begin to encounter the magnitude of the soul as the form of the body. We see that human beings are the union of time and eternity. Our bodies are in time, but our souls are raised above time because we can see the past, present, and to some extent the future.

Sight, which stands distinct and is achieved over distance, is the privileged sense that reminds us of our difference from the animals and our nearness to the angels. We are more than an accidental difference on the scale of animal sensory powers. Other mammals do not question their existence, they do not ask transcendent questions. Humans are the only earthly creatures who see the forest for the trees. Our vision opens us up to questioning ourselves, others, and the nature of time. We are alone in our capacity for this type of vision. The difference between us and all other creatures is not being more advanced and on the same ladder but being on a different scale altogether. Humans are a different *kind* of being than all other creatures, owing to our image and likeness to God. If we were on the same ladder as other animals, we would be at a disadvantage. Our sight is unremarkable and a mediocre tool for processing the world. We cannot see clearly in the dark like the birds of prey who accurately track and capture their meals. Nor can we swivel our eyes like chameleons, each in opposite directions, to process two different sensory experiences. But our sight is far more remarkable than any other animal's because it signifies our co-creating of heaven.

Our senses are not passively bound to our environment. In the image of God, we transcend that passivity and actively make worlds within worlds. Our sight calls to mind history and time with every vantage. We place objects within their narrative. Sight cannot help but connect all, revealing to us glimmers of the invisible thread that connects all moments, underscoring all reality. This is why the blind man who asks for sight in the Gospels paradoxically sees more than many with physical sight. Human sight is not lost with the loss of physical sight. Physical sight is a portal into immortal vision, as time is a portal to eternity and flesh to the resurrected state. With St. Paul, *"we look not to the things that are seen but to the things that are unseen. For the things that are seen are transient, but the things that are unseen are eternal."* Human sight is only ever fully realized when it sees that it desires the vision of the unseen: *"By faith he* [Moses] *left Egypt, not fearing the king's anger; he persevered because he saw him who is invisible."* Sight calls to mind the illumination of that invisible thread connecting and transfiguring all things in the radiant vision of sanctified love. *"For now, we see in a mirror dimly, but then face to face."*

> The Son is the image of the invisible God, the firstborn over all creation. For in Him all things were created: things in heaven and on earth, visible and invisible, whether thrones or powers or rulers or authorities; all things have been created through Him and for Him. He is before all things, and in Him all things hold together.
> —Colossians 1:15–17

Taste

> The house of Israel named it manna, and it was like coriander seed, white, and its taste was like wafers with honey.
> —Exodus 16:31

> My son, eat honey, for it is good, yes, the honey from the comb is sweet to your taste; know that wisdom is thus for your soul; if you find it, then there will be a future, and your hope will not be cut off.
> —Proverbs 24:13–14

> Taste and see that the Lord is good; blessed is the one who takes refuge in him. Fear the Lord, you his holy people, for those who fear him lack nothing. The lions may grow weak and hungry, but those who seek the Lord lack no good thing.
> —Psalm 34:8–10

> But we see Jesus, who was made a little lower than the angels for the suffering of death, crowned with glory and honor; that he by the grace of God should taste death for every man.
> —Hebrews 2:9

> And the woman said to the serpent, "We may eat the fruit of the trees of the garden; but of the fruit of the tree which is in the midst of the garden, God has said, 'You shall not eat it, nor shall you touch it, lest you die.'" Then the serpent said to the woman, "You will not surely die."
> —Genesis 3:2–4

> Can something tasteless be eaten without salt, or is there any taste in the white of an egg? My soul refuses to touch them; they are like loathsome food to me.
> —Job 6:6–7

> I tell you, not one of those who were invited will get a taste of my banquet.
> —Luke 14:24

> They came to the chief priests and the elders and said, "We have bound ourselves under a solemn oath to taste nothing until we have killed Paul."
> —Acts 23:14

Through taste we consume and take within ourselves the foods that will sustain our being. Taste is violent, visceral, *and* one of the most pleasurable exercises of life. In taste, we move beyond the contemplative gaze of sight and hearing. We are also far past an ethereal imbibing or inhaling of the spirit that comes with smell. The closest, touch, even as it dominantly grips and grasps, cannot devour the other the way in which taste initiates such power within us. St. Jerome's version of Job 6:6–7 is quite striking: *"Can anyone taste that which being tasted produces death?"*

This unique sense positions us in a direct placing of the other on our lips and in our mouths. It goes even further than direct placement, it forcibly breaks down the elements of the other with our teeth and tongues. We reshape, dissolve, texturize the substance, then swallow, ingest, and digest it. We make it a plaything that becomes one with our bodies, feeding our flesh and blood and vital organs. We deconstruct its structure and order and accost its lifeforce. We empty its being to nourish our own. The tongue itself also capitalizes on another sense, touch. It presses and rolls the sustenance around the mouth and against the back of the teeth. It also makes use of the world of sight, smell, and hearing within its presence. The wine tastes of the straw we hear crushed underfoot, it tastes of the inhaled fragrance of honeysuckle, fire, tobacco, nuts, oak, the crispness of autumn. Through them we find ourselves in a clearing in a forest where such tastes inhabit and intermingle. The honeysuckle and the oak remind us of backyard play in the late warm days. The straw and the tobacco bring us elsewhere into the past, of grandfathers, farms, and where cool sunsets each arrive earlier than the day before. Taste does not solely contemplate these memories but grafts them into our flesh. Taste breaks each piece down into the minutest of forms so that the entirety of their substances can be assimilated into us, so that we concretely, viscerally, violently, become the other *as other*. Or rather it becomes one with us.

Taste reminds us that, compared to the angels, we take the longer way to spiritual contemplation. Our way never sheds the richness of embodiment. We may take-in others into our minds and souls, but we do so *through* the body. The soul orients itself as united to the senses. The transcendency of spirit, much like prayer and grace, must be consumed and ravished within our being.

> While they were eating, Jesus took bread, said the blessing, broke it, and giving it to his disciples said, "Take and eat; this is my body." Then he took a cup, gave thanks, and gave it to them, saying, "Drink from it, all of you, for this is my blood of the covenant, which will be shed on behalf of many for the forgiveness of sins. I tell you, I will not drink from this fruit of the vine from now on until that day when I drink it new with you in my Father's kingdom."
> —Matthew 26:26–28

Christ alone fulfills our need to consume the spirit, to understand sanctity through taste. His *sacrificial* gift, His total self-emptying fulfills and marvelously exceeds what has always been signified within taste. *"My tears have been my food day and night, while people say to me all day long, 'Where is your God?'"* In taste, we empty the other to nourish ourselves; we consume the other to complete what is lacking in us. But no taste ever emancipates us from the cycle of need. What we have consumed is now absent; we have emptied the food of its essence, and while it is within us, it is only transient fullness revealing itself as disintegrating form. This consumption as consummation of the other achieves its climax and fulfillment in the Eucharist. The Eucharist involves a twofold sense of consummation: (1) the consumption of the outward appearance of the host, the accidents of bread and wine, which remains and which the senses readily perceive and (2) the consumption of the substance of the bread and wine transformed into the substance of Christ's body and blood. In the consumption of food, we desire a substantial change, but never fully achieve retaining the fullness of the thing consumed. We must empty what is consumed to engage it, losing its substance in the process. And when we consume, our accidents change—we may become heavier, thinner, fuller—but our substance remains the same. In taste, we long for the consumption as consummation of the other that transforms our entire beings. At Communion, we are infants only just born. Each of us desires the pure spiritual waters, the drink that quenches our thirst, *"Taste and see that the* Lord *is good."* We hunger to taste the substance that causes within us essential substantial change, the one that realizes the inklings of heaven on earth.

Christ's eucharistic *self-emptying* completes what taste has always desired but could never achieve. The texture, look, smell, the accidents of the bread and wine (taste, texture, appearance) do not change. We handle them as we did before. But the substance does change. It tastes like bread and wine, but it is Christ's body and blood. In transubstantiation, Christ turns taste upside down. It now fulfills what taste has always signified but could never clearly convey or capture. Christ offers us not accidental change but a taste of substantial change, filling us with the hope for the resurrection of our bodies. When we consume the Eucharist, we experience a twofold layering of tastes. In tasting the bread and wine *as bread and wine*, we are reminded of time and memory relegated to a recollection of past events. In this first form, we taste and confirm our bondage to accidental change. This confirms our link to the passing and dying world. But like human sight, which sees without physical sight, all our senses point beyond themselves to the hope for the resurrection. Taste has always pointed past itself in yearning for something that could substantially fill us. Something that could fill us, not merely temporarily satiate. In tasting of the body and blood of Christ, time and memory are recovered and glorified in the substantial change that offers us the only true taste of Life itself. This taste brings us into the very body of the resurrected state. We adore the Eucharist. Let us lower ourselves onto our knees to receive as birds do from their mothers. It dissolves on our tongue. It is crushed between our teeth, subsumed into our substance, as we are subsumed into it. This second form of tasting is not a recollection or remembrance of a past event. It is the foundational re-collection of Being, Truth, Goodness, Beauty, and salvation. It is making present what *Is*, Christ's total self-emptying re-collected, re-membered in us. The Eucharist is contemplated within the violence of *eros* colliding with *agape*. It is life bleeding out agonizingly into death, and death resurrected joyously into life. This act of tasting re-collects the passion of our Lord. This consumption as consummation completes within us the paschal mystery. In tasting, we are physically re-collecting Christ's death and resurrection.

> For I received from the Lord what I also passed on to you: The Lord Jesus, on the night he was betrayed, took bread and when he had given thanks, he broke it and said, "This is my body, which is for you; do this in remembrance of me." In the same way, after supper he took the cup, saying, "This cup is the new covenant in my blood; do this, whenever you drink it, in remembrance of me." For whenever you eat this bread and drink this cup, you proclaim the Lord's death until he comes.
> —1 Corinthians 11:23–26

Summary Remarks on the Senses and Paradise

> O God, you are my God; earnestly I seek you; my soul thirsts for you; my flesh faints for you, as in a dry and weary land where there is no water. . . . My soul will be satisfied as with fat and rich food, and my mouth will praise you with joyful lips.
> —Psalm 63:1–5

If we are to hope for the resurrected state with enduring persistence, then we must rediscover the wealth of indications housed within our five senses. History is a long list of misappropriated senses. We are told to abandon our senses in the forms of suppression and subjugation, which have their merits in only the rarest of forms. Or the human person is expected to surrender to the senses *because* the world is viewed as purely material. The senses lose their transcendency and are mere biological drives alienated from their spiritual appetite. The reduction of the senses to materialism is more often than not the response to a loss of sanctity. The abandonment of the senses, for all its wildly adamant desire, fails to find any real home on earth because everywhere *is* the body and the carnal. Our soul is not housed in the body as water is contained within the glass. The flesh is permeated with soul. Bypass the senses, and one bypasses the spiritual altogether. There is no faith without the flesh. *"That which was from the beginning, which we have heard, which we have seen with our eyes, which we looked upon and have touched with our hands . . ."*

Sin has always been about senses stripped of their proper end and value. Sin will forever be the denial of the spiritual status of the senses. It reduces the senses out of their place in eternity and forces them into the closed loop of biological drives.

> They [the idols] have mouths, but cannot speak, eyes, but cannot see. They have ears, but cannot hear, noses, but cannot smell. They have hands, but cannot feel, feet, but cannot walk, nor can they utter a sound with their throats.
> —Psalm 115:5–7

Every sin of the flesh is a sin of disembodiment, no matter how much the body is used, devoured, centralized, and manipulated. Such sins are the promise of heightened senses, when what is on offer is dull and worn-down motivations that approach nothingness. Our senses need to be realized within a powerhouse reality. We act from eternity when we act in time and our likening power is relatively higher than the angels' likeness to God. Our senses reveal a magnificent nuptial quality and activity. The senses marry us to the divine reality in the world. It is crucial we recover the dignity and charge of these nuptial-bound senses within the journey to our permanent home. The senses enable us to experience what Christ offers to us as our Bridegroom. Christ offers a transcendentally sensual fidelity as prefigured in the erotic lover and beloved union of the Song of Solomon:

> How beautiful is your love, my sister, my bride! How much better is your love than wine, and the fragrance of your oils than any spice! Your lips drip nectar, my bride; honey and milk are under your tongue; the fragrance of your garments is like the fragrance of Lebanon. A garden locked is my sister, my bride, a spring locked, a fountain sealed. Your shoots are an orchard of pomegranates with all choicest fruits, henna with nard, nard and saffron, calamus and cinnamon, with all trees of frankincense, myrrh and aloes, with all choice spices—a garden fountain, a well of living water, and flowing streams from Lebanon. Awake, O north wind, and come, O south wind! Blow upon my garden, let its spices flow.
> —Song of Solomon 4:10–16

Each of the five senses unveils the perfumed pattern of the Bridegroom transfixing our lives, transposed with all newness, promise, peace, and sanctification.

- Smell completes itself in inspired breath, which climbs into the center of our chests. Scent enters into the place where the Sacred Heart resides. We who inhabit His fragrance of creation, His perfumed passion redeemed, inhale the God that happens within us daily. Our physical bodies rhythmically remind us, every moment, of the breath of God that brings us to life. Our lives are ever in need of the exhalation of the Holy Spirit.

- In touch, we seek to cross the divide that separates things, beings, objects. We look towards becoming one in being with the other and desire that touch accomplishes a nuptial level of union. If only we could touch the cloth that our Bridegroom wears, all shall be made well.

- The exquisite power of hearing as obedience to God's call is a receptive surrender, where every lover is the beloved and every beloved is the lover. We, the bride, surrender to the Bridegroom of Truth, Goodness, and Beauty. In hearing we must turn our whole being to distinguish the word from the idle noise and chatter.

- Sight achieves its union with the Bridegroom through the recognition of distance and nearness. Sight is the privileged sense that unveils how much closer we are to the angels than to the animals. It also acknowledges the vast unseen lengths that must be traveled before we can arrive at the wedding of the Lamb. For Christ is *"the image of the invisible God, the firstborn of all creation."* Human sight, united to but exceeding physical sight, immerses itself in the unseen netting that encompasses all things and desires the invisible to be made visible. *"There will be no more night. They will not need the light of a lamp or the light of the sun, for the Lord God will give them light."* This is the sight aligned with faith as *"the substance of things hoped for, the certitude of unseen things."*

- Taste reveals to us the physical contemplation specific to human beings born to the *longer way* of spiritual life. Our spiritual contemplation arises through consumption and ravishment. It is to be moved along our teeth, within our mouths, around our tongues. We tasted the forbidden fruit and lost our earthly paradise. Now our taste seeks to consume and reconstitute what is lost, a new Eden. Taste unveils the desire for Christ's *self-emptying*. In and through it, we desire a substantial change, but it is impossible to retain the fullness of the earthly things consumed. What is tasted is consumed, emptied, and has nothing left to give. Only Christ restores the savor in the salt, only the God-Man has something left to give when tasted, consumed, utterly emptied and abandoned. *"Jesus answered them, 'Destroy this temple, and in three days I will raise it up.'"*

Our mystical body is fulfilled in the resurrected state. Only through our senses does Christ come home. We make home in Christ's flesh Who first offers Himself to us in His home identical to His flesh and blood.

> For we know that if the tent that is our earthly home is destroyed, we have a building from God, a house not made with hands, eternal in the heavens. For in this tent we groan, longing to put on our heavenly dwelling.
> —2 Corinthians 5:1–2

We *smell* and breathe in the fragrance of His word. We *hear* His call, necessitating our entire bodies turn towards Him. We *touch* His garment so that all things shall be well. We *see* the invisible with the eyes of faith. We *taste* His *self-emptying* love, which alone satisfies all hunger. If we forsake or shortchange the senses, we reduce the glorified state to a recitation of empty, well-meaning but deadly platitudes. Our flesh permeates our soul. This reality is glorified in Our Lord's agony on Golgotha. And it is illuminated even further in the ecstasy wherein Doubting Thomas places his fingers in Christ's wounds. The disciple is touching the spiritual crucible which clarifies the mystery of our senses transubstantiated through faith and grace.

> "Unless I see the nail marks in his hands and put my finger where the nails were, and put my hand into his side, I will not believe." . . . "Put your finger here; see my hands. Reach out your hand and put it into my side. Stop doubting and believe." Thomas said to him, "My Lord and my God!" Then Jesus told him, "Because you have seen me, you have believed; blessed are those who have not seen and yet have believed."
> —John 20:25–29

Bypass the senses, and one bypasses the cross and resurrection altogether. There is no in-between state, the glorified body does not perniciously reside halfway between body and soul, but inhabiting neither. Christ is our Body and our Bridegroom. He is no mere go-between.

> Let not your heart be troubled: you believe in God, believe also in me. In my Father's house are many mansions: if it were not so, I would have told you. I go to prepare a place for you.
> —John 14:1–6

There is no faith without the flesh, only disembodied homelessness, hell itself.

14

Stairway to Heaven

What Does Christ Tell Us about the Resurrected State?

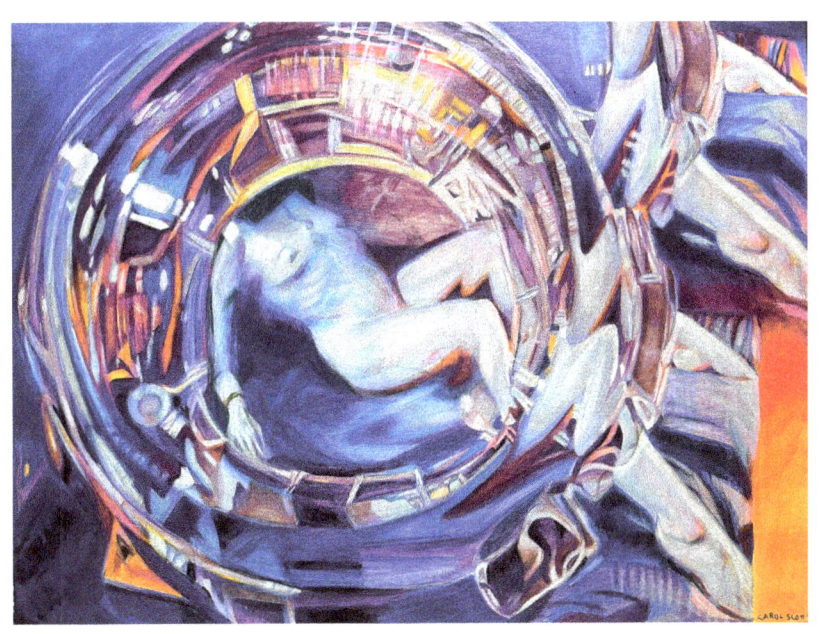

Redolent Blue, by Carol Scott

Goodnight love maker, dream maker, the stars swirling in melting cup overflow
Tears of your face, tears of time, the hour of joy is yet to come

Close me and open, maker of dreams, enamored sleep, chambered you descending the stair

My caught heart rests one fathom below where you are in gold of lower sea

Dream for me life taker, love maker, song of you sunk down, dying in bliss

My prayers are made of night sky, hidden in longing, years of my face
Untouched you, the hour of joy is yet to come

Stars were made to dream on, shooting wishes, resting on the moon
Struck by the sun, casting shadows of memories
Banking my desires, jumping fun you came

First dawn of the day you wake, cause of future hope, co-create grace
Good morning love maker

   —"Goodnight Love Maker," by Carol Scott & Caitlin Smith Gilson

> Blessed are the pure in heart, for they will see God.
> —Matthew 5:8

WHAT CAN WE NOW justly understand regarding the type of embodiment we will have in the resurrected state? What glimpses have our five senses provided? What we surmise must be united to humility. Although our inferences have worked to wipe away much of the easy, wish-fulfilling hope and disembodied speculation, it is still a looking through the glass darkly. And it will always be this way until the light that *is* Christ, that *is* the beatific vision, illuminates in paradise *our* embodiment *through* His own. "*I have come as Light into the world so that everyone who believes in Me will not remain in darkness.*"

Christ's incarnation leads us by way of a twofold mystery. His body is on the way with us, a wayfarer. His spirit is an immediate and full *comprehension* of divine realities. How are these two experiences, intrinsic to the God-Man, authentically related within His supreme *self-sacrifice* on the cross? If this mystery is not properly oriented, we cannot approach the God-Man. We would not have a resurrection worthy of belief, and we would have no foundation to glimpse our resurrected state. Everything is at risk. Paradise has always been played for the highest of stakes. Both aspects are essential to Christ; otherwise, we would not have in Christ the second person of the Trinity. We would have a quasi-human, quasi-divine go-between and not the true Mediator. Christ must be the goal and source of the beatific vision in order to enact the message of salvation. Otherwise, He is not the Word made flesh.

This unique status to Christ prompts us to ask interesting and difficult questions. For example, does Christ hope? Christ experiences abandonment and cries out, "My God, My God why have you forsaken me?" The experience of this terrible longing is consistent with a broken hope, a hope once present and fading. Christ is one of us. This is essential to His shepherding of all humanity. All human beings hope. But to save us, His immediate and full *comprehension* as God must also be present. Otherwise, He wouldn't have the power to save us. As no human can save himself. God does not hope. He is the *source* of hope and in possession of all hoped for realities. From the beginning of His conception, Christ as *fully God* had the Divine completely. Christ *as fully God* is the source of faith. He did not have faith regarding anything, because He knew all things fully. Therefore, he had not the virtue of hope. But Christ as *fully human* had hope for such things as He did not yet possess. Christ *is* truly dying on the cross, *is* truly seeking our salvation, Christ is truly surrendering to the Father. Salvation has not yet been fulfilled. Therefore, Christ hopes for these goods He did not fully possess pertaining to His perfection, such as immortality and the glorified body.

To approach our embodiment in the resurrected state, we must dwell on the mystery of how Christ comes to God as *fully* man. Christ's petitioning the Father is the image to which our likening power must attach itself. He could not authentically petition God as the *most* fully human person, yearning for salvation, if His divinity renders such action play acting. The person of Christ is the union of two natures, divine and human. The properties of both natures always remain seamless and unconfused. The uncreated is always uncreated and the creature remains within creaturely limits. It is impossible for any creature to comprehend the divine essence. The infinite is not comprehended by the finite. This means that the soul of Christ does not comprehend the divine essence. The soul of Christ can and does hope. Christ has a true wayfaring desire. On the one hand, He could not petition His Father, as more truly human than any human ever was, unless He *is* in full comprehension, *is* the image of the Word. Christ's soul knows all things in the Word. For it is befitting human beings to know in the Word. And we see more perfectly *through* the Word. No beatified intellect fails to know in the Word. Christ knows in the Word all things existing in time and all our thoughts, of which He is the Judge. Christ knew us not only in divine knowledge but also of His soul's knowledge, which it possessed in the Word. Christ on the cross is the apex and estuary of all human-and-divine desire for the invisible to be made visible and tangibly present.

In the agony of the passion, Christ is exiled. He can no longer find a home in the Father. The homelessness Christ experiences is the essential reckoning that must occur for Him to make His body paradise for us. He is barred from home and feels abandoned. This is the archetype of the dark night of the soul for the mystics. Christ entered complete darkness. He no longer experienced the All through His infused contemplation. In Christ's passion and death, the radiance of his entire soul was most powerfully present, but no longer experienced by Him. Jesus was deeply united with the Father, but the union consisted of agony, anguish, blood, and tears. He was near God through sheer absence. All of this must occur to overcome death and make His wounds the way to heaven for us.

The God-Man is not a set of dueling unrelated natures held together by forced dialogue. There can be no dividing line cut down the middle of

Christ. There is no partition of the curtain, when convenient, that distinguishes His intellectual and embodied experiences, some pertaining to God and others pertaining to humanity. It cannot be a managing of when His divine status takes dominance, as if in a perpetual competition with His longing human nature. Either Christ is *fully* human and *fully* God or our whole desire for the resurrected state is grounded on lamentably faulty foundations. Again, everything is at stake.

For St. Thomas, Christ is fully united to the consummation of the divine plan, identical to the source of all hope. He does not possess the virtue of hope as if hope is an end other than Himself. But crucially, Christ is also able to possess *and* exercise hope through human longing for completion. Christ's hope again materializes in the things He did not yet possess, befitting of the human soul, which acts from a potential good to actual good. The soul is always informing the body, and Christ's body is deteriorating and dying on the cross. Christ, as the supreme human, is hoping for what He has not yet achieved—immortality and the glorified body—while He experiences its visceral contrary, namely spiritual and physical decomposition.

Christ, as the only human born to die, experiences hope through the longest and most arduous of ways. He experiences hope only by first casting and framing its impossibility within His putrefying flesh where, let us recall, human souls are *not* made separately from their bodies. The soul is *not* supposed to separate from the body. It does so because of original sin. Christ experiences the longest way to hope through the terrible agony of dying, when it appears all hope has been conquered. True hope cannot be fulfilled after original sin and before Christ's incarnation. We may have wishes, desires, fantasies, dreams, but the bridge to hope, like the bridge over the river Kwai, has been thoroughly blown apart. To recover paradise for us, Christ must *become* the bridge, must *be* our hope fulfilled.

Christ is consumed by abandonment. He endures the entirety of the ruptured soul unnaturally wrestled apart from the body through death, which cannot realize hope. He made Himself the hope for heaven by first enduring the totality of its abandonment and lostness. He entered death and then, out of nothing, became its new ground. Christ as God is Existence Itself. When creatures live and act, they do so on the reality of God's creation. We act out our lives on God's Being. But Christ does not act out his existence on any other existence but Himself! When he is abandoned, He is inflicted with a greater loss than any other human being could ever be or imagine. We may deny God, but we still act out that denial on His existence and creation. To reacquaint us with the hope wholly abandoned in the ruptured human essence, Christ must experience the loss of creation entirely. He must open a new avenue of existence for us. We removed the grace of immortality because we were unwilling to receive it. There is no way to claw our way back, no structure of hope that can fulfill our desire. If Christ in His humanity is going to give human beings hope in the resurrected state, He must self-empty everything that He *is* as the body of all existence, from which all finite acts and choices spring, to begin again the movement of life from a potential good to an actual and fulfilled good. He must abandon the original framework that our free will has refused. All was lost in original sin. Christ's passion does not shortchange this terrible reality.

Christ's divinity enabled Him to experience the lengths of our ruptured essence as homelessness and hopelessness. It terrifyingly allowed Him to move past the safety net of our finite nature. All our choices are within a preceding set of finite acts, all returning us to creation as the ground we act on. When we make choices, we never leave the presence of God's Being. Our leap is never as risky as it seems. The greatest risk, the highest stakes are always played out on the cross. The highest risk is on every Good Friday, from the beginning till the end of time. Redemption does not work by fiat, by simply returning what we freely chose to forsake. Our hope for immortality that reflects the unity of soul and body was lost. The strange and uneasy state of the separated soul attests to those heartrending consequences. If Christ is to make possible what within us is impossible, he must go by way of impossibility and death. There is no longer any potential to actualize that glorified body, for we had chosen death. There were no finite potentialities left for Christ to actualize. There was no way for Christ to save us as the fireman rescues the child from the burning building. Christ is no mere superman using the tools already around Him to save the day. He does not actualize our potential in the same limited manner as the superhero actualizes the potential for greater strength or speed through already existing strength and speed. Christ as *fully God* knew all of this. Christ as *fully human* accepts its consequences with an acceptance that goes so far beyond anything we can imagine. If there is no potential for immortality because we have removed our link to the image that actualizes this, Christ does not undo our choice.

In essence, there is nothing left with which to unstick the tape and replace it as before, there is no way to undo the misplacement. There is no situational possibility because there is no ultimate actuality that can fulfill that hope for immortality and the glory of the body. The actuality was lost to us and with it the structure to actualize our potential for immortality. Not even a situational possibility remained. Christ's self-emptying is exhausting and terrifying. His *"My God, My God why have you forsaken me?"* holds all the cards to our resurrected state *because* it holds *no* cards. God created out of nothing, and Christ, to save us, creates once again out of nothing on the cross. Christ, too, must go by way of nothingness but of a different kind altogether, one of abandonment. This is not the nothingness of creation that inaugurates all our possibilities. This is the nothingness of death which ends all life, where every option is extinguished. He must resurrect by forming out of this total abandonment the new ground of possibilities. Christ can only hope for it to be formed. All control is abandoned, all framework is lost. That was the *only* way Christ could proceed in His rescue mission. Should the miracle happen and life can come out of death, then it is God's grace, and the impossible is realized *through* Christ's body. This is why there is no heaven that exists apart from Christ's flesh and blood. It is why He resurrects with His scars and why death is now our greatest of friends.

Without Christ's martyrological love, there would be only fantasy and disoriented desire for our immortality and for the glorified body. On the cross, Christ alone transforms that unfulfilled wishful yearning (which is all it would ever be without Him) into genuine hope. To do so, Christ completes the deepest and darkest night of the soul, the longest of longer ways, by placing Himself at the center of that ruptured essence, that violent separation of our body and soul, due to our original sin. Christ accomplishes hope by creating a new path to actualize Goodness, Truth, and Beauty. He makes the nothingness of abandonment and death the foundation to actualize eternal life. Christ's flesh is the prayer and plea of unanswered prayers answered because they are one with his flesh and blood wholly abandoned and unanswered on Golgotha.

Whatever is good and excelling in us must be in Christ as foundational. Christ is the source and image to which our likeness tends. Christ embodies how we hunger for salvation while certain of its promise through the God-Man.

> And He was transfigured before them; and His face shone like the sun, and His garments became as white as light.
> —Matthew 17:2

15

Christ Enters into Us

THIS IS THE KEY TO OUR GLORIFIED BODY

Magnum Opus, by Carol Scott

The scent of fresh sea air in autumn has a way of reminding me of you
    In spite of the feeling that this chill in sun has a sadness to it, a
    foreshadowing of winter suns barely strong enough to warm the days,
    the long dark December nights
Still I am brought into view of you, the passing thought remains within me
You bundled up immune to cold, all body warm, the scent of that freshness
The sea close at hand, the bells always on time always a surprise
The sun still beating through the windows, into the deep of autumn, all of
    this has a way
    Of transporting my senses back, giving all my senses back to you
This passing thought stays within me for the time being I am looking out at
    the passing scene without my senses yet feeling everything
How is it that the scent of fresh sea air, in this autumn at this moment
Has a way of reminding me of you? We have never walked the beach
    together
So many things we have not done, it is enough only to be sleep loving sleep
Two presences dreaming for the other, into the other, all the good giving
    the good
The sun beating through your window, into the deep of autumn, the passing
    thought
Sits within me, I think of late nights, how the later afternoon lays down its
    shoulders
Into late night, the tablecloths are blowing up and down, barely fixed to
    their existence
With well-placed glasses, this scene, the comedy of it, the joy of being, the
    frenetic need.
Has a way of bringing me back to days with you. but more the nights, My
    toes stuffed now under the covers, making trenches, blanketed hills. the
    cold,
Come to think of it, it is cold, so many passing thoughts, my limbs feel
    separate from my body the encroaching winter, the sea water still has its
    salt on my skin
My hair still drips with it in waves, the thought of hot shower, eyes closed,
    your home
The sense of being between two seasons, this finds me longing for you

    —"The Passing Thought," by Caitlin Smith Gilson

All This, and Heaven Too

CHRIST HAS CREATED THROUGH His death the new realm by which we act out our immortality. We must take a closer look at how our senses are in relationship to death if we are to glimpse a vision of our resurrected state. Christ resurrects with His scars; this signifies that death paradoxically dilates our understanding of the glorified body.

> Perhaps in that kingdom we shall see on the bodies of the Martyrs the traces of the wounds which they bore for Christ's name: because it will not be a deformity, but a dignity in them; and a certain kind of beauty will shine in them, in the body, though not of the body.
> —St. Augustine, *The City of God*

Here we encounter the Platonic paradox never to love our lives so much that we render them unworthy of living. The best of who and what we are is discoverable in the extending, underlying, encompassing, sanctified dying within daily living. It is the look and touch and aspect of this dying that is not ignored but transformed in the resurrected state when Christ overcomes the world. Death is not to be viewed through the lens of morbid and obsessive fear or obsequious reverence. Instead, the strong and vital desire to engage life most vigorously and within the Beautiful always means a natural, almost unthought, but dwelt-in, readiness to die. *"For whoever wants to save their life will lose it, but whoever loses their life for me will find it."* Such a person is nourished on the nectar of Christianity, whose love radiates from Christ's breathing and gestures. This person is capable of such magnanimous beauty because Christ is a friend to death because His existence is markedly *self-emptying*.

> Let the same mind be in you that was in Christ Jesus, who, though He was in the form of God, did not regard equality with God as something to be exploited, but emptied Himself, taking the form of a slave, being born in human likeness. And being in human form, He humbled himself and became obedient to the point of death—even death on a cross.
> —Philippians 2:5–8

The human body in the resurrected state would be a living artform. Each glorified body would have the keys to understanding the manifold layers of each person's story. Our stories would illuminate from the skin, shine from the face, transmitted in the warmth of touch, and in the gaze that does not hide, it only reveals love. Every glorified body would be brightened and clarified through intimacy with the beatific vision. We would experience the lover-and-beloved relationship unique to each person in Christ. The resurrected state would be the story of every soul—its scars, stretch marks, hardened palms, furrowed brow—visibly overwhelmed by grace. The elusive completion of our earthly meaning, which dying intensified and distilled but could not communicate, is fulfilled with the outpouring of Christ's *self-emptying*. His relentless love knows us better than we know ourselves. His death remakes what is possible, gifting us with a new path to glory. Through Christ's death, our experience of dying becomes the very key to express what death has shaped and distilled within us. In dying we discover the throbbing need to utter the mystery, the incommunicable that has always laid at the center of our chests. The realization of our dying brings us to this climax but then strips us of the possibility to express what resides innermost in us. Death leaves us mute, lifeless, unable to communicate. Our anguished, spasmodic souls gasp, unable to express what is most dear. But in union with Christ, we can speak the heart and soul of us that once lay too deep.

> When the time comes to you at which you will be forced at last to utter the speech which has lain at the center of your soul for years, which you have, all that time, idiot-like, been saying over and over, you'll not talk about the joy of words. I saw well why the gods do not speak to us openly, nor let us answer. Till that word can be dug out of us, why should they hear the babble that we think we mean? How can they meet us face to face till we have faces?
> —C. S. Lewis, *Till We Have Faces*

Our glorified bodies dramatically unveil Christ at our left and at our right, above us, below us, in the midst of us, inside of us, radically fulfilling our co-creation of paradise. The armor of God that we place upon ourselves in life is not a struggle against flesh and blood. It is against the evils that degrade the body's magnificence to carry eternity in time. More still, this armor is nothing other than flesh itself, Christ's flesh and blood permeating us. Christ's crucifixion is also an infixion: a yielding of our bodies to the Word being placed, inlayed, infused within them. The nails and lance that scar Christ pour forth His vital essence and fill the Word within us. This overflowing fills our scars, the lines on our faces, the cracked hands, all the signs of death, disease, decay, old age. All of these things simultaneously reflect our personhood and our failure to transmit and communicate what lays most truly within us. Christ's loving self-emptying is an abundance. Heaven as Christ's body is now ours, suffused with His in the resurrected state. This filling up of our scars does not cover over our imperfections, for like Christ we, too, rise with our scars. It perfuses them with radiant Truth, Goodness, Beauty, and Love. This gift of self-emptying communicates the greater glory of the journey of a human life. The divine and eternal is discovered in daily life in our flesh and blood. Our glorified wounds reveal the magnificent reality that our likening power to God is greater than the angels! Through Christ, we are more perfected rising *with* our scars. Those signs of death now transmogrified in His. Life is a prelude to this permeation. We hide in Christ's wounds in life preparing to experience Christ filling our own wounds in paradise.

We are united to Christ in our glorified bodies. Christ fills each of us. We experience that gift with others in heaven. What sex and procreation attempt to communicate is fulfilled in the glorified state. Earthly intimacy attempts a permanent union where we transmit ourselves fully into the beloved. But death does us part, and no earthly love can complete its desire for union. When Christ fills our wounds (once the sign of death and loss) with His overflowing body, we can finally achieve that intimacy, that complete union with every glorified soul. Every story we began and could never finish is now read across our bodies in their hallowed perfection. Our resurrected state is not discoverable by foolishly inoculating ourselves against death. It is in the breaking up of the flesh with time and age that we make room for this loving entrance of Christ into us. Our glorified bodies love life. They love the holy death in our living beings that is Christ's immortalizing armor of flesh and blood. But those blind to the gift that Christ has made for us through the transfiguration of death see only the scars, the disease, and the suffering. For the one who can see, the joyful suffering unto death makes way for the most beautiful of bodies, filled with the perfume of Christ.

> In the Messiah, in Christ, God leads us from place to place in one perpetual victory parade. Through us, he brings knowledge of Christ. Everywhere we go, people breathe in the exquisite fragrance. Because of Christ, we give off a sweet scent rising to God, which is recognized by those on the way of Salvation—an aroma redolent with life. But those on the way to destruction treat us more like the stench from a rotting corpse.
> —2 Corinthians 14:16

Our Faces

> My heart says of you, "Seek his face!" Your face, LORD, I will seek.
> Do not hide your face from me.
> —Psalm 27:8–9

    In the resurrected state, our faces would take on the character of every age. They would even possess the ages we did not reach. God knows all future contingencies, the roads we travelled and did not or *could* not travel. Christ as the head of our bodies suffuses us with the radiant truth of every face. We would look at our mothers with every face that we are, that we were for her, every face that had heightened her life, her experience and ours, and more. We would gaze and be gazed upon. We would transmit in every gaze all their loving completions because Christ's *self-emptying* is within them. Our eyes would take in what alone would satisfy. *"As water reflects the face, so one's life reflects the heart."* In our glorified bodies, we would look with Christ's eyes so that our own face would beam from His face Who saves.

    "O LORD God of hosts, cause my face to shine; and we shall be saved." Our faces would be Beauty Itself since we would be filled with the divine light that makes Beauty seen, the source that establishes due proportion, rendering us lovers of beauty. We would become the very light of glory. Colors would exceed in brightness, enticing every sense to enjoin. The luster of grace forfeited by sin and death would be magnificently restored by the divine Artisan who makes our bodies the very art of time revealing eternity. The resurrected state is a nuptial union. Through the bride's radiant face, we encounter Christ, our Bridegroom:

> Your cheeks are beautiful as the turtle dove. You must not give an earthbound meaning to this coloring of the corruptible flesh, to this gathering of blood-red liquid that spreads evenly beneath the surface of her pearly skin, quietly mingling with it to enhance her physical beauty by the pink and white loveliness of her cheeks.
> —St. Bernard of Clairvaux, *On the Song of Songs*

Our Breathing

> When you hide your face, they are terrified; when you take away their breath, they die and return to the dust. When you send your Spirit, they are created, and you renew the face of the ground.
> —Psalm 104:29–30

In the resurrected state, our breathing would call to mind inhalation, which occurs both in dying and in the act of creation. As we die, every breath gasps for more oxygen, the body fights to receive sufficient lifeforce. Because the beatific vision is an infinite end, an inexhaustible intensity, our breath would correspond in a transformed likeness. Each breath would take more, would joyously grasp for more, and our exhalations would transfix our fellowship with the Holy Spirit.

Each breath would be more pleasing, without the prior one lacking anything or being any less pleasing. The struggle for more oxygen would be transposed into the infinite access of the spirit as alpine and clear. Every breath would be world-forming for, like God, our exhaling would be creative, it would co-create paradise, forming life and landscape, citadels carved by the rhythm of each breath. Our breathing would be always in rhythm with Christ and with our dearly beloved, glorified family.

Our Senses: What Mary Magdalene & Doubting Thomas Share through Touch

> "Don't cling to me," Jesus told her, "Since I have not yet ascended to the Father. But go to my brothers and tell them that I am ascending to my Father and your Father, to my God and your God."
> —John 20:17

> "Put your finger here; see my hands. Reach out your hand and put it into my side. Stop doubting and believe."
> —John 20:27

These two passages appear to put the Resurrected Christ in contradiction. Christ urges a shocked and ecstatic Mary Magdalene, the first to witness Him alive right outside the tomb, not to hold on to Him, whereas Doubting Thomas is invited to place his fingers within the wounds. How do we authentically reconcile the *"do not cling to me"* with the far more intimate act of placing oneself within Christ's lanced sides? What do these two mysterious and essential passages, particularly their tension, tell us about our senses in the resurrected state? Mary Magdalene is given the most privileged task of telling the others what she has witnessed. She must transmit to others what is unbelievable, and, as a woman, she would seemingly be the least credible witness, the least effective of messengers for Christ to choose. It is for this very reason that we recognize the power of Christ's self-emptying into us through an overwhelming unification of the senses.

Christ elevates Mary Magdalene in her task by ensuring that she knows with certitude, tangibly, without physical clinging and touch. Her witnessing of Christ evokes presence and contact more penetrative than earthly touch. Her body is infused with that power. She will run to the other disciples and every sense will leap to proclaim that Christ has risen! She is filled with His touch *through* sight.

> All night long on my bed I looked for the one my heart loves; I looked for him but did not find him.
> —Song of Solomon 3:1

Mary Magdalene *has* found the one her heart loves. And Christ gifts her with the first sighting of our Risen Lord. But her touch, which still embodied the yearning and distance of the Old Testament, must be transposed. Her senses must be transformed to realize the new covenant of Christ's flesh and blood. *"Woman, why are you crying? Who is it you are looking for?"* This new touch is signified when Mary does not recognize Christ until He calls her name. His calling transforms her recognition, unifying all her distinct senses as one with Christ as heavenly teacher. Christ's love self-empties into all our senses as realized in Mary Magdalene. In a paradisical transfiguration of synesthesia, His resurrected word is *touched* when it is *heard*. It is *tasted* when it is *seen*, its perfume is as substantial as touch. It is heard because tasted, inhaled as it is seen, and in touching we have tasted. There are no fragmented senses, but a unity corresponding to our body as one in being with His heavenly body.

There is urgency in Christ's *"do not cling to me."* Mary Magdalene corresponds to Christ's completed self-emptying. Mary's sight of Christ *is* also touch, taste, hearing, smell. Sight as the most privileged of earthly senses is synonymous with the urgency to spread the good news. In Christ's interaction with Mary Magdalene, we realize that our senses now leap forth. All are united in the sensuous new life that has been washed brilliantly white with the blood of the Lamb. Christ's pouring entirely of Himself into us has undone the blindness, deafness, muteness, the insensitivity to touch and dullness of taste that fragments our experience of the world and our ability to love others.

Christ's interaction with Mary Magdalene unveils *self-emptying*, which unites the senses as one in Christ. Doubting Thomas's interaction with Christ reflects Christ's *filling* of our wounds, our failures, and disbelief. Our Lord fills us up with the Word. What is weak is made strong. Our fatal flaw becomes the foundation for courage and endurance. As Christ rises with His scars, so do we. Our senses are not only dramatically unified through Christ's self-emptying, but it is the filling up of our failings, scars, defects. They are not magically erased but permeated with the Word Himself. In the breaking open of our flesh and the weakness of our senses, we discover the greater glory of Being. Through Christ, Thomas's doubt becomes the vessel of strength, that glorious impertinence to place his unworthy fingers within the flesh of God Himself! Remember that we had forsaken possibilities when we had chosen death. We had closed off life. When Christ saved us, He does not save by magic but by what remained, which was the dead-end of death. Our Lord made death impossibly the greatest possibility. He filled the death in each of us with His death *as* resurrection. His filling up reflects death overcome, not erased, in the glorified state. This permeation means that we carry death transfigured within us as the very presence that glorifies our bodies. Heaven is not a homogeneity, where each person sees the same, hears the same, touches the same, looks the same. Christ offers a personalist revolution to heaven. He permeated our weakened senses so that the weakness itself is the vehicle of transcending glory:

> The Lord said to me, "My grace is sufficient for you, for my power is made perfect in weakness." Therefore, I will boast all the more gladly about my weaknesses, so that Christ's power may rest on me. That is why, for Christ's sake, I delight in weaknesses, in insults, in hardships, in persecutions, in difficulties. For when I am weak, then I am strong.
> —2 Corinthians 12:9–10

Christ's *self-emptying* and *filling up* of our wounds are entirely unified. Each aspect presents a different emphasis of Christ's sacrificial love that unveils our co-creation of paradise. Each signifies two fundamental aspects of our senses in the glorified state. Mary Magdalene's experience of Christ's *self-emptying* signifies the defragmentation of our senses, the power that enables each one to signify the whole. To see Christ is to taste Him, to hear the lover is to embrace Him. The *filling up* of Doubting Thomas's wound of disbelief confirms that this unity of the senses in the glorified state is not a power placed atop our senses. It is not a superhuman power indifferent to our earthly senses or outside of our life experiences. The glorified body is won *through* our senses, achieved *through* their weakness, filling their dying, transfiguring their failings. Christ condescends to become united with my eyes, my hands, my lips, and tongue. This is the greatness of Christ infusing His body to ours. Because every glorified body is infixed with Christ's *self-emptying* presence, our senses in paradise would cross every divide. In our glorified bodies we now forever touch Christ's garments, and through this permanency all has been made well.

In the resurrected state, our senses are penetrative, each evoking the other, fulfilling unity. The touch of another's arm or face enables one to love the other with such intimacy as old friends. The unveiling of shared experience within touch is not as isolated ideas, facts, or descriptions of past events, but as a total unitive experience of the incarnation. In paradise, all things are made one and overwhelmed with goodness and sanctity. The hearing of praise in paradise would elicit the taste of nectar, the sight of the beautiful moments of one's child, both recollected and unseen, now taste of manna. The forgiveness spoken would take on the scent of every sweetness, bread pulled apart, freshness of ocean and tide, domestic and exotic, known and unknown. Our senses in paradise fulfill what is sensed on earth when we embrace, when we kiss, when we seek furiously to touch something more than skin deep, when we inhale the garment of the lover now dead and seek to reclaim with our very smell and breathing the life of the beloved. The bride will grasp her Bridegroom and not let go.

16

Lovers in Paradise

What Becomes of Friendships, Fellowships, Marriages

The Lovers, by Carol Scott

Dearest friend of mine
The moving image moves on
And I am woven into the soft
The deeper memory
The unearthed first death
The only one to survive

There will be decades that pass
Life has its lonely passage
Its corridors haunt without end
Ending in no room and no place
But I am living within the sanctity
Of your heart grieving its flowers
Into mine grieving time

There is no time here but expression
The texture of your living descending
As fingers dipped in oils of the Cross
Made with the body
Dwelt in the spotless soul
Anointing me in the beauty
Of your life

Loving you
Knowing the timeless heart
That lives inside
Your time-bound smile
I could fade into the forgotten
And remain the one made of sand
Stretched across the seas

Your words
Any of them
All of them
Have a way of landing in me
As long-traveled albatross
Flighted over oceans
To find ground

All This, and Heaven Too

I rest in the thought of this
The image of that flight
A silent muscled contraction
Extending shadows
Over motionless stretches of sea

I could cry
Thinking of you and this
This image of you
Soaked smile of mind and memory
The sponged wine fell into my lips between stone and sky
I hold onto you as waters unmoved
—"The Friendship in Christ," by Caitlin Smith Gilson

> From quiet homes and first beginning,
> Out to the undiscovered ends,
> There's nothing worth the wear of winning,
> But laughter and the love of friends.
> —Hilaire Belloc, "Dedicatory Ode"

THE IDEA OF GENUINE fellowships—not reduced to mere usefulness or convenience, but those that bring out the divine in the friend and lover—would seem to be a natural fit in the resurrected state. Friendship and spousal union were ordained from the beginning. "*The LORD God said, 'It is not good for the man to be alone.'*" Christ came as Bridegroom, offering the greatest of friendships. "*No longer do I call you servants. . . . I have called you friends. . . . You did not choose Me, but I chose you.*" The three persons of the Trinity are the prime foundation for a purely loving relationship. They are a fellowship of perfecting communion.

We ask not only of the important re-uniting with the spouses, children, and friends we had on earth but of the process of *becoming* friends, of *falling* in love, of *discovering* the other, of the joys that *spark* fellowship and nuptial union. We learn from Jesus that there will be no new marriages in heaven. He relays this to Sadducees who seek to trick Him regarding the marital status of a woman who had been widowed multiple times. Are we to assume that discovery, invitation, union, and fellowship are past us in the resurrection? Why would Christ be the Bridegroom, and we the bride of Christ, if we are not called to a union of love so intimate it can only be described as nuptial? What, then, would discovery of love look like in the resurrected state?

We wonder also about the hope of salvation for those persons, sometime friends and loved ones, who helped another along the way to salvation but in themselves turned away God. What happens to those who estranged themselves from friends and family who desired their genuine happiness? Where are those people who exclude themselves from paradise? How would it feel for those who have made it to heaven should they be able to look upon such an alienated soul? Our fallen state initiates a range of alliances and types of unions, both noble and ignoble. What remains of those earthly bonds in the resurrected state? We must consider those many relationships that suffered damage throughout life from sin and shortsightedness. What do we make of good relationships briefly encountered but never fulfilled due to time, change, and death? Is there a process of completion and discovery, particularly since God knows all things, including the outcome of every road not taken? This would be a particularly pressing question regarding the abortion of the unborn and the children whose lives are tragically cut short. More still, how do our earthly unions play a part in the nature of paradisal unions? Do fellowships bridge the gaps in salvation, help to recover what may be lost? How are they to be envisioned or transformed? Or is the process of discovery completed at the moment of death? Strangers enter paradise already *as friends*, as a community bonded in the *friendship* embracing the beatific vision.

> Finally, brothers and sisters, rejoice! Strive for full restoration, encourage one another, be of one mind, live in peace. And the God of love and peace will be with you. Greet one another with a holy kiss. All God's people here send their greetings. May the grace of the Lord Jesus Christ, and the love of God, and the fellowship of the Holy Spirit be with you all.
> —2 Corinthians 13:11–14

Old and New Love

St. Francis Xavier wrote the following letter to his dear friend St. Ignatius:

> You say in the excess of your friendship for me, that you would most ardently wish to see me once more before you die. Oh! God alone, who looks into the heart, knows how vivid and how deep an impression this dear proof of your affection has made on my soul.

> Each time I recall it—and that happens often—my eyes involuntarily fill with tears; and if the delightful idea that I could embrace you once more presents itself to my mind (for, however difficult it might appear at first sight, there is nothing that holy obedience cannot accomplish), I find myself for an instant surprised by a torrent of tears that no power can arrest. I pray God that if we are not to see each other again while living, we may together enjoy in a happy eternity the repose never to be found in this life. It is all over; we never shall meet again on Earth otherwise than by letters; but in Heaven—ah! We shall meet face-to-face. And then with what transport shall we not embrace one another! Who, indeed, can tell the transports which two virtuous friends will experience for each other eternally in heaven, after having here below loved each other unto perfection, and verified the saying of Holy Scripture: "A faithful friend is the medicine of life and immortality; and they that fear the Lord shall find such a friend."
> —St. Francis Xavier, *Letters* (in Blot, *In Heaven We'll Meet Again*)

From this ever-timely letter on friendship, we witness those bonds that are faithful companions on the royal road of suffering and sanctification. Let us dwell the possibility of renewed and new unions in paradise by reflecting on four indicators that support a robust discovery of friends, family, spouses, and loved ones in the resurrected state:

- God has never been a withdrawn or enclosed Being. Paradise is unity with His image, which is by nature Trinitarian and relational. God makes possible all relationships.

God is not a windowless, withdrawn Being. If this were the case, there would be no relevant discussion of paradise. Nor are we in a one-way relationship with a divine principle which we can strive towards but itself is cordoned off, enclosed, and separated in its own eternal perfection, having no view towards us. Paradise is grounded on the infinite and overflowing foundation of God as Trinitarian. God is Love Itself in communion with all things. It is far more unrealistic to imagine our participation in the beatific vision to be something *other* than, or opposed to, friendship. Friendship is understood as the dilation of the other person towards the fulfillment of the good and the possession of happiness. Friendship must necessarily dwell in all genuine loves, from fellowships to spousal love. Remember, Christ offers us friendship. At its best, friendship is joyful praise and uncovering of the divine life within our friend. When you love others, you desire their happiness with a thirst equal or greater than your own desire for happiness.

The best friendship desires Christ for the friend. Christ alone can satisfy our thirst for happiness.

- Human beings cannot access their humanity without relationships that are perfected in virtuous friendships.

Without human relationships and unions, we would be spiritually impoverished, blocked off from our history and essence. We cannot fulfill our personhood without the friends who take us in as we take them in, interiorizing and exteriorizing ourselves and others. This act reveals us as transcendent beings who long for the impossible but essential image of the infinite. This interiorizing and exteriorizing of ourselves and others is the netting that incarnates the world for us. It helps us realize the dignity of our nature made in the image and likeness of God, Who is relational Love Himself. It would be a defective reality if the blessed should be alienated from each other in paradise. It would be analogous to modern neighbors, each in his own house, occasionally coming outside to see what commotion has transpired on the streets and proceeding to rattle off the usual forms of polite conversation. But nothing beyond that. No real intimacy or love. The blessed are united in the image of the divine as supreme love. The blessed will be enveloped in divine friendship itself, becoming, in that uncreated light, friends of the highest order. Each infused with the image or archetype to which all earthly virtuous friendships tend.

> When God is "all in all," then He will be the completion of every human desire, both realized and unrealized. Our union will be an endless love, a praise that never tires, an activity which is itself intimate and shared by all.
> —St. Augustine, *City of God*

- Christ does not offer servitude but friendship, made possible through Love identical with His flesh and blood.

"A servant does not know his master's business," but we are each called to know Christ, to have that audacious intimacy of friendship. Christ, Whose body itself is heaven, and Whose incarnation brings heaven into earth, offers us nuptial friendship. He chose us. He gifts us through His flesh and blood with the *love* of an immortalizing union. Fellowship begins in our relational response to our creation. This relationship is magnified in the Holy Trinity and exercised in Christ's self-emptying and filling up of our scars with His love. It would be a contradiction, a paradise unworthy of

our longing, if that self-emptying communion somehow dissipated. It is essential to the co-creation of the architecture of the resurrected state. Christ infuses His word within us, and His word is self-emptying. This means that we are never closed off. Sin and ignorance close us off, but in that overflowing abundance that Christ offers us, we are opened to friendship and love once again.

- It would be a terrible contradiction to possess the glorified body and enact that glorious state void of friendship.

The resurrection of the dead is supported in the relationship of the soul and body. The body is *for* the soul as the soul is *for* the body, each perfects the other. Together they illuminate the human person. Embodiment always evokes relationality intrinsic to human beings. To have a body means to claim space, to take up a specific location within a multitude of points and features in the world. Sensory embodiment cannot help but mean a relation to other beings by virtue of recognizing ourselves as nearer to or farther from other beings. The human body is always engaging what is in its surroundings as more or less like itself. More still, our physical bodies are always connected to transcendent meaning. The experience of physical tiredness, for example, provides a template to express spiritual apathy or dismay. The feeling of being full and happy after a good meal, for instance, provides a foundation for describing fulfillment in other aspects of life. The human person tends towards union and fellowship. We experience this tending from our most basic physical states to our transcendent desires. How would it make any sense that our corruptible earthly bodies, *"sown in dishonor,"* be capable of engaging the beauty of friendship and the desire for eternal life, but our resurrected and incorruptible bodies are less capable? Our glorified bodies would be far more adept at engaging the true friend, the greater lover, and the most blessed of fellowships. Friendship would be vigorously intensified in the glorified state, not vitiated. The happiness of the blessed will increase after the resurrection. Their happiness will then be not only in their souls but also in their bodies. The joy of our souls in the glorified state will increase in intensity. Our souls will rejoice not only in their own good but also in that of their glorified bodies.

None of us is certain to be one of the blessed who resurrects in glory with Christ. But should this greatest of blessings be gifted to us, then we *can* be certain that the most beautiful of unions would permeate the mansions of paradise. But fellowship in the resurrected state is not a reductive repetition of the best of earth. Christ's self-emptying offers us graces reflective of friendship and spousal love on earth, but it is of another and higher order altogether. Paradisal friendship, united in the resurrected Christ, is the archetypal image to which all virtuous earthly unions tend. Viewing paradise as a mere continuation of earth undermines the resurrection. But conceiving friendship in the glorified state to be something so far beyond the senses, alienated from all earthly meaning, is also missing the point. Earthly friendships provide an indication, a genuine trace of its source; but no earthly friendship is ever the archetype. Friendship in the resurrection is not a likeness to earthly friendship by way of derivation or mirroring. That would not quench our thirst or satiate our desire for completion and fulfillment. Instead, friendship among the blessed is an immensity grounded upon the infinite and intensifying discovery of Trinitarian Love. Such a friendship would be the greatest adventure, the most profound discovery, the shimmering estuary of *love* where all *eros* and *agape* resolve themselves at the wounds and feet of the Bridegroom.

In paradisal friendship we would be entirely available to love what is discoverable *as lovable* in all the creatures, beings, and persons. This supreme disposition exudes from us, glorified in the uncreated light of God. And since our friends in heaven act on the body of God, Who realizes all persons as inexhaustibly lovable, they would become the *greatest* of friends. Each would unveil the endless joy of discovering God's infinite love at the heart of the beatific vision, inflaming our own hearts. Discovering old and new unions, friendships, and loves in paradise manifests the spiritual dowry Christ gave to us, clothing us in fine garments, adorning us with jewels, which are synonymous with His flesh, blood, fellowship, brotherhood, and friendship.

Is There Sex or a Union in Its Place?

> Let him kiss me with the kisses of his mouth: for your love is better than wine. . . . Draw me, we will run after you: the king has brought me into his chambers: we will be glad and rejoice in you, we will remember your love more than wine: the upright love you.
> —Song of Solomon 1:2–4

The issue of sexual union in the afterlife is an admittedly curious question. It becomes an increasingly pressing one when we acknowledge the promise of the resurrection. Our final happiness is not the disembodied vision of God in heaven but the overwhelmingly robust resurrected life. We are obligated, albeit in a limited manner, to approach the potential nature of the glorified body in such a state. What is emphasized from heaven to the resurrected state is the fullness of the human person. The two states are entirely united in the glory of God, yet they are and *must* be differentiated meaningfully. Otherwise, what would be the point of this gratuitous addition of the glorified body? If our resurrection is inessential, a spiritual complement to an already completed state, we end in an anti-climax, a devalued incarnation. The glorified body would be the bit of parsley to cleanse the palate at the end of the main course.

What is human experience like in heaven before the resurrection, in our disembodied state? Certainly, it is not unconscious nor is it the feeling of being awake that occurs with bodies refreshed in the morning. It is a peace-filled knowledge, a sleep in which the will is at rest and the intellect is fully in the divine vision. Everything in this resting knowledge is identical with the True, Good, and Beautiful. God Himself acts in the place of the body, making up the difference, dramatically overcoming the lack of embodiment. But this is the experience of perfection *via* the fully true dream. It is a heaven of ecstatic dormition and grace-filled rest. When we grow up, we lose our ability to sleep, to rest as children do. We are fitful and let the world of fallen forms separate us from sleep, which prepares us to resurrect refreshed and indefatigable.

> Children don't even think about being tired. They run like little puppies. They make the trip twenty times. And, consequently, twenty times more than they needed to. What does it matter to them. They know well that at night (but they don't even think about it) they will fall asleep in their bed or even at the table and that sleep is the end of everything. This is their secret, that is the secret to being indefatigable. Indefatigable as children. Indefatigable like the child Hope. And always to start over again in the morning.... It's this same bottomless sleep. As continuous as being itself.... It's in this same sleep that children bury their whole being. Which maintains, which creates for them every day new legs, their brand-new legs. And also that which is in their new legs: new souls. Their new souls, their fresh souls. Fresh in the morning, fresh at noon, fresh in the evening. Fresh like the roses of France. Their souls with the undrooping collars. This is the secret to being indefatigable. Just sleep. Why don't people make use of it. I've given this secret to everyone, says God, I haven't sold it. He who sleeps well, lives well. He who sleeps, prays.
> —Charles Péguy, *The Portal of the Mystery of Hope*

Lovers in Paradise

In heaven we recover the sleep that our waning and lost innocence forever craves up to the moment of death. In its disembodied state, we experience the great restful knowledge (dormitive-cognition) that children encounter. This is the rest that gives them the appetite of discovery, joy, play, and newness to help them survive the age where rest is increasingly replaced with resignation. It is this resignation that signs our death warrant, that confirms we do not have the power to resurrect, that we have nothing within us to refresh ourselves everlastingly. Should we be refreshed it comes from beyond us, not from our strength, and that grace must fill us again with its rest.

> Your dead will live; their corpses will rise. You who lie in the dust, awake and shout for joy, for your dew is as the dew of the dawn, and the earth will give birth to the departed spirits.
> —Isaiah 26:19

Heaven is meaningfully different from the resurrected state. Resurrection necessitates the refreshment of the mind, soul, and body to be risen from the dust, to be recovered and renewed, becoming transformed and indefatigable. This does not occur to persons who do not have within them the sleep that is as bottomless and continuous as God Himself. The eternal light that gives us perpetual rest in heaven refreshes and prepares us to put on the flesh of the new person. In God everything is timely: *"There is a time for everything, and a season for every activity under the heavens."* The season of the resurrection is the time for perfection in wakefulness. *"Awake, sleeper, and arise from the dead, and Christ will shine on you."* Clothed in Christ, we experience that beatific vision through our glorified bodies. We awake to our bodies that walk and breathe, smell and touch, whose profoundly unified senses are given privileged participation within the eternal.

With such a vigorous accounting of fellowships, unions, and friendships in the resurrection, one that does not shirk the dignity of the body, we may surprisingly but rightly turn to the status of sexual intimacy in paradise. What becomes of that most intimate of carnal unions? Do our glorified bodies leave sexual intimacy behind since its earthly goal of procreation is no longer relevant in paradise? There is no longer death, and thus no need for generation to compensate for the deficit in life. Because mortality is wholly overcome and absent from the equation, there is no inner motivation to preserve our lives through sustenance which staves off death. And there is no place for sexual intimacy to augment the population. Earth is complete, God's judgment is final, there are no new persons to be created. The powers to sustain our lives and the population would be fruitless in paradise. The logic appears to be without flaw. Paradise presents a radically different situation for the body. The body is transformed, along with the soul, to be enjoined to the beatific vision.

The idea that paradise would include an abundance of sex that bears no fruit, brings no life, drastically undermines the earthly and glorified bodies. Such a union is wholly unfitting. It is something all too pedestrian. All too easily accomplished here on earth. It is more of the stuff of hell and its self-enclosed egos. It is objectivizing the body of the other person for the advantage of the self to hide its own failure to love. This view of sex in the resurrected state is clearly opposed to the sacredness of love-*making*. It denigrates the powerful purpose to bring new life. What pleasure could an unfulfilled act of sexuality have in relation to the beatific vision?

Or, to play devil's advocate, does this view smack of shortsightedness? There is an intensity of intimacy furiously sought to be attained in sexual union. At least, there is *more* to be reflected upon regarding how sexual intimacy is transformed into the resurrected state. Our glorified bodies mean we have eyes and ears and voices to praise God. Our senses are infused and enriched with the blood of the Lamb, which makes God exceedingly more visible to our senses. It is wholly at odds with the concept of resurrection that we would be resurrected as eunuchs or, more drastically, void of sexual organs altogether. Every part of our body through Christ's *self-emptying* and infusion is glorified. What becomes of our sexual organs? Every aspect of our flesh and blood is raised, transformed. Each wound is no longer a defect. Each of the senses and every body part praises God. Again, what must we genuinely understand about our sexual organs and of human intimacy? Are we simply to bypass them as inconvenient along the way to a neutralized, disembodied spirituality? But this seems to be unwise and inauthentic given how Christ beckons us with nuptial language. Our Lord calls us into the intimacy of the bedchamber as Bridegroom to His bride.

There is no shame or lust in paradise. Each person is resurrected to his or her unique and individual stature. Even the unborn, who die in their mother's wombs, will rise. Each uncovering his or her uniqueness through conformity to Christ's resurrection. Christ alone preserves and elevates the unique differences of our embodiments and spiritual appetites. What, then, could be an authentic and beautiful way to dwell on how sexual intimacy is meaningfully transformed and elevated in paradise? In sexual intimacy, lovers seek to conquer the divide and unify as one in joy and ecstasy. The resurrected state is not a static end but a dynamic embrace of God's infinite fountain of creativity and love. Wouldn't it be strange not to possess an active, intense union within that radiating vital force, the transcendent source of all earthly love-*making*? Shouldn't we act on that divine love-*making/creating* experience in a way that reflects not only our embodied but our resurrected state? We must be mindful not to express our intimacy as if identical to the angels. While we possess a spiritual nature, we are not to be pure spirits like them. This does not befit our natures. If we were, the resurrection would *not* be the state of our ultimate happiness. The state of our separated soul would be sufficient. What we seek in paradise is what is glimpsed in love-*making*.

> nothing which we are to perceive in this world equals
> the power of your intense fragility: whose texture
> compels me with the colour of its countries,
> rendering death and forever with each breathing
> (i do not know what it is about you that closes
> and opens; only something in me understands
> the voice of your eyes is deeper than all roses)
> nobody, not even the rain, has such small hands.
> —e. e. Cummings, "Somewhere I Have Never Travelled"

Much of the glory and the folly of our human lives and decisions revolve around sexual union. And ultimately around the nuptial embrace. Additionally, the procreative power to help create another life has always been the core of human existence. The tension between sex and enduring union is at the heart of human spirituality. In sex, there is the chief desire to push past death and into immortality. *"May your fountain be blessed, and may you rejoice in the wife of your youth. A loving doe, a graceful deer—may her breasts satisfy you always, may you ever be intoxicated with her love."* In climax, the little death deterministically resolves itself each time. It cannot complete the union. Our intimacy is grounded in the Edenic exile. But it is mystically rehabilitated in Christ as Bridegroom. While we are living, sexual intimacy resides anxiously and uneasily in between. This tension is the beautiful and tragic act of the fallen world.

> Love is what is most terrible and tragic in the world. Love is the child of deceit and the parent of disenchantment, love is the consolation in disconsolateness. Love furiously seeks through its object something that lies beyond it and, not finding it, despairs. . . . In love we seek to perpetuate ourselves on Earth only on the condition that we die, that we surrender our lives to others. The humblest little animals, the lowest living beings, multiply by dividing, splitting

> in two, ceasing to be the singles they once were. And every act of engendering is a ceasing to be what once was, a splitting, a partial death. Perhaps the supreme delight of engendering is nothing but a taste of death in advance, the rending of one's own vital essence, ... because only in others can we become eternal. There is, without a doubt, something tragically corrosive in the depth of love in its primitive, animal form, in the unconquerable instinct that impels a man and a woman to mix their bodies in furious embrace.
> —Miguel de Unamuno, *Treatise on the Love of God*

Sexual love is the most tragically corrosive act in the world. It draws all like moths to a flame. It indiscriminately presents to those made of earth and clay the promise of *completed* immortality of soul *and* body. In sex, we dive into the other, we encircle briefly that transfixing and transposing of the soul. We glimpse the transfigured redemption of flesh and blood through the rupture in temporality that places the united lovers somewhere between time and eternity. Love-*making* gives us a moment in climax of becoming fully the beloved. We become the beloved not only immaterially but in a way that would distinguish us from the angels, specifically reflecting human beings as soul *and body*. It gives us a foretaste of Christ's self-emptying. In communion, Christ accomplishes becoming one with us both immaterially and, crucially, physically. But no human sexual act completes what it promises: bodies die down, souls retire into themselves, the union separates because it cannot sustain itself. Love-*making* is furiously drawn out through history, engendering more life to try again and again to free itself from death. Only Christ, as Bridegroom, completes this powerhouse tragic desire within sexual intimacy. Our Lord fulfills the making of love, or love-*making*, in the highest order. Our pro*creative* power finds its image *only* in God's creation. God formed us from the depths of the earth and created our inmost beings. *"I praise you because I am fearfully and wonderfully made."*

It seems that there must be a genuine role for the meaning of sexual intimacy within the resurrection. What we understand of love-*making* in paradise transcends what we understand of it as sex on earth, but not in a way that all identity to it is lost. Otherwise, why stress that we resurrect into full glorified bodies if the sexual organs have no transcendent role to play? To deny the role of sex lends to the rejection of any relevant role for the senses in paradise. Our hands that touch Christ's wounds, to feet which carry us through the co-created mansions of paradise. Why do we need any of the senses in the resurrection if God can already be experienced immaterially in heaven? But grace *perfects* nature: the whole soul is *for* the whole body and the whole body is *for* the whole soul. This wholeness attaches itself to the relationship between the glorified soul and body. There is no genuine resurrected state unless the *whole* body is understood to be glorified in God's exceeding grace. Virtuous love-*making*, the relentlessly gentle and gently relentless coupling of one lover to the beloved, is perhaps the most foundational act on earth that points to the desire for resurrection. It enters transiently but unsustainably into the orbit that alone overcomes death. What is always sought is the nuptial union of gentleness and firmness, of love being made and given. This is only fulfilled in the self-emptying of the Bridegroom to His bride.

> What gentleness, my child, what firmness in gentleness, what gentleness in firmness.
> One and the other bound indissolubly, one forwarding the other, one setting off the other, one upholding the other, one nourishing the other. Gentleness entirely armed with firmness, firmness entirely armed with gentleness. One enclosed in the other, the other enclosed in the one, like a double stone in a double fruit of firmness. A gentleness all the better guaranteed by firmness, a firmness all the better guaranteed by gentleness. One bearing the other. For there is no true gentleness except founded on firmness. And there is no true firmness except clothed in gentleness.
> —Charles Péguy, *The Mystery of the Holy Innocents*

We could never comprehensively understand how the role of sexual intimacy is transformed in the resurrection. But we can reasonably recognize that love-*making*—as forming, creating, shaping flesh into flesh—provides on earth the dearest and painfully sublime reflection of the glorified body. This acknowledgment must also cause us to pause on how our bodies are experienced in the resurrected state. Perhaps paradise is the true climax hinted at and yearned for within all love-*making*? In the glorified state we finally complete the task, making ourselves unending vessels of love. We fill into overflow the beloved, as the other fills us, as Christ has filled us. This intimacy is not a mirror image or mere continued reflection of earthly union. Aquinas is right to reject that the need to populate and sustain our bodies through food and health has any purpose in sustaining paradise. But this does not negate their roles altogether. What is reflected in our glorified bodies should be *our* bodies and souls glorified. Paradise has its own love-*creating*, love-*enshrining*, love-*permeating*, love-*exuding*, love-*radiating* form of love-*making*. This, again, is not a *reflection* of earthly love-*making* ever in battle with death. Paradisal love-*creating* is the image to which all earthly likeness reflects. Its capital image is Christ, the Bridegroom beckoning us with *every* summit of *every* joy within *every* completed end to His bedchamber.

Our resurrection made manifest through Christ. What we smell are the perfumes of Christ. What we hear is music united to His word. We touch and taste *with* His flesh and blood, which are rivers and oceans, estuaries, mountains, fruits, wine, undreamt landscapes all co-created through our flesh and blood. In paradise, no part of the body is triggered because it lacks something. Because there is no lack in paradise, there is no need for what embodiment offers us. Our senses are not needed because they do not *need* to point out what we do not possess for peace and survival. We are in the complete possession of our beatitude. Yet, this lack of need does not indicate their lack of essential presence in the resurrection. It is essential that the earthly body, which for so long hungered for what it lacked, be raised in its fullness. The senses are glorified in their completion. This is achieved because we unite with our true other half, the truly complete person, Christ. Christ completes our striving natures. He completes all our desires for unity and relationship.

What becomes of sexual intimacy in paradise is a magnificent completion. Our glorified bodies possess sexual organs not because we *need* them to complete something lacking in us. Our whole bodies are glorified because each aspect is a critical indicator of our desire for our permanent home. Love-*making* emphatically distinguishes us from the angels. It confirms the union of our soul and body. The resurrected state completes the relentless incompleteness of every earthly striving, every frenetic sexual union, which could never outwit time, sin, weakness, and death.

> I'd like to weld you together and join you into something that is naturally whole, so that the two of you are made into one. Then the two of you would share one life, as long as you live, because you would be one being, and by the same token, when you died, you would be one but not two in Hades, having died a single death. Look at your love, and see if this is what you desire: wouldn't this be all the good fortune you would want?
> —Plato, *The Symposium*

There would not be sex in paradise because such an action would not be paradisal. All union, intimacy, completion is accomplished and held in fullness in the climax of the beatific vision. In the resurrected state one's entire body and soul would be bathed in union with the Bridegroom. There would be no parting, no separation, no need to enter the other to furiously renegotiate a union. There is no more panting for streams of water, no more tears searching for God. The union is held forever at its climax. This definitively contrasts all earthly sexual intimacy, whether it be virginal and chaste, erotic, or mystical. Each earthly *eros*, no matter how transcendent, must find itself incomplete, unable to self-empty entirely into the beloved and be wholly infused by the beloved. At their most sanctified, these earthly, incomplete intimacies relish the sweet and throbbing wound from our Bridegroom's absence.

> I saw in his hand a long spear of gold, and at the iron's point there seemed to be a little fire. He appeared to me to be thrusting it at times into my heart, and to pierce my very entrails; when he drew it out, he seemed to draw them out also, and to leave me all on fire with a great love of God. The pain was so great, that it made me moan; and yet so surpassing was the sweetness of this excessive pain, that I could not wish to be rid of it. The soul is satisfied now with nothing less than God. The pain is not bodily, but spiritual; though the body has its share in it, even a large one. It is a caressing of love so sweet which now takes place between the soul and God . . . which was to me a greater bliss than all created things could give me.
> —St. Teresa of Ávila, *Life of St. Teresa*

It is this absence as nearness that compels prayer, surrender, love*making*, and all the glory and folly of human intimacy. We seek to hold once again the sweetness and redolent union of the divine arrow driven into us. We long for the resurrected state, where every beginning of our own selves would have no end. Each aspect of who we are would be enveloped in Christ. His *self-emptying* is an infusion within us. He has permeated us with the Word. With Doubting Thomas, we have placed our fingers and our bodies within Him. This is why when the Pharisees are fasting, Christ as Bridegroom with his attendants did not fast. He was *with* them, and because he is united to them, there is abundance, completion, joy. Sex and every earthly intimacy are reflections of fasting. Sex is not the opposite of the abstinence and hollowness that forges through history and unveils centuries of longing since the Bridegroom went away. Much of earthly intimacy cannot recognize itself as fasting and is confused, thinking it can satisfy itself. Genuine nuptial union knows it does not have its own power to fulfill itself. It needs the marriage blessing, the grace of God. Craving the beloved is an act of spiritual fasting. And this is why there is such profound resonating truth to "theology of the body" and to the proper dignity of sexual union. We must come to terms with this spiritual fasting rather than delude ourselves into pseudo-fulfillment. True sexual enlightenment is the realization that we are always in need of the one person, Christ, Who completes us as His own.

> John's disciples and the Pharisees were fasting; and they came and said to Him, "Why do John's disciples and the disciples of the Pharisees fast, but Your disciples do not fast?" And Jesus said to them, "While the bridegroom is with them, the attendants of the bridegroom cannot fast, can they? So long as they have the bridegroom with them, they cannot fast. But the days will come when the bridegroom is taken away from them, and then they will fast in that day."
> —Mark 2:18–20

17

Closing Miscellany

Play, Laughter, and Animals

Susie Mermaid, by Carol Scott

All This, and Heaven Too

There is something about you, I could say it is an invisible thread, some sort of netting
Far below any reach connecting me to you, but it is not that, it is other
Not for a moment do you leave my thoughts, what I mean is that you do not escape
The underlying thought, the constant undying record that must be me when all is said and done
The sound wave below sound, where I live as a soul inhabiting the world beyond Eden
You are grafted into me as body healed with another, but it is more
Even as I work and play and become distracted by life, subterranean you are
Taking root somewhere, more than my mind, more than my essence, even more than my heart
But what is more than the heart, is it the teardrop, the swelled and fallen tear
More than word, a compact perfect tear, consummate angelic spirit, fastened into me
It is not that, it is something more, I could say you are in my blood but I already have that
Are you the inner gilding of my veins and arteries so that you move seamlessly with my pulse
Beating in time with me,
Even if in all poetry, it is the Beautiful, that your being moves in concert and mine with yours, it is yet something else
Its joy could only be exsanguinated Cut away from itself
A whole body reduced to thorns, Calvary and the Cross . . .
But I have always felt its trace, this trail of ecstatic wandering
Unknown seductive grace, I do not know what inhabits you, I think it fills you this place
Before my first thought, I was made of it, this place
There is something about you, somewhere to you, a place in you, that is more than every waking Thought that I have ever had, so I keep thinking about you, what exactly I think about, in a way it does not matter, it is that you live below my tongue, all speech emptied into the love of you

—"Of Love and God," by Caitlin Smith Gilson

Closing Miscellany

On Play . . . with a Little Laughter in the Midst

> Then our mouth was filled with laughter, and our tongue with shouts of joy; then they said among the nations, "The LORD has done great things for them."
> —Psalm 126:2

THAT INTIMATE UNION WITH Bridegroom is best understood through earthly play. Play is the enactment of the sacred. It is a realm invested with meaning because it is lived in *unison* with the good in the divine joy. We manufacture right and wrong from often petty, worldly ways where vice is dressed up as virtue. We accept a mediocre level of kindness as acceptable. But play overflows with filial bonds forged in the love that anticipates paradise. Play is a unique virtue. It is not a trying and difficult obedience but virtue *as virtue-exemplar*, filled with beauty of our remnant original innocence. For we do have a remnant innocence in us. If it were simply absent, the agonizing descent of our fallenness would no longer possess its sting. Play prepares us to recognize that sting and to live virtuously even if we must remain within the dryness of an obediential recognition of the Good. *"Blessed are you who weep now, for you will laugh."* The playful heart preserves us to endure that dryness. It is the secret companion to grace and the interior meaning of Christ's words: *"Suffer the little children, and forbid them not to come unto Me, for of such is the kingdom of heaven."* None of us can make an alternative path to what grace freely yet essentially gives. This does not mean that we cannot place ourselves within its hope. Play gives us that disposition for grace.

The holiest appetite for transcendence is play-filled love. We are the clay shaped only by the Beautiful, the Good, and the True, becoming the vessel most ready for grace. A play-filled heart merges its personhood into the glory of the moment. Time is not merely paused or forgotten but rather finally lived in its wondrous fullness. We experience Christ's loving permeation, which fills us with newness, promise, and joy. Our senses are awakened to hear, see, smell, taste, and touch with the reverence of a Creator for its creation. In this merging of time into the finally lived present, we have a foretaste of how we co-create the architecture of paradise with Christ. We are in play with Christ forming all things. We become apprentices to the Master Architect. And Christ is delighted with us every day. His happiness is His most secret wisdom yet so very radiant. We play before Him at all times and in all times. We create heaven in play:

> The LORD possessed me in the beginning of his ways, before he made anything from the beginning. . . . I was with him forming all things: and was delighted every day, playing before him at all times; Playing in the world: and my delights were to be with the children of men. Now therefore, children, hear me: Blessed are they that keep my ways. Hear instruction and be wise, and refuse it not. Blessed is the man that hear me, and that watch daily at my gates, and wait at the posts of my doors.
> —Proverbs 8:22–23, 30–34

In C. S. Lewis's *The Lion, the Witch and the Wardrobe*, we witness the terrible betrayal and cruel death of our Christ-figure, Aslan. But after having just come back to life and knowing that much more strife and suffering is ahead of Aslan and the Pevensie children, Lewis presents the most audacious decision to have Aslan romp and play with the children. Here Christ communicates His self-emptying not in the sheer seriousness of the passion but in His abundant joy. Play is entrance into the kingdom of heaven. In play, Christ begins to fill us up and raise us into paradise. Nothing other than the ecstasy of heaven can combat the power of hell. Our joyful hearts must exude the perfume of Christ to overwhelm the stench of sin. Play communicates more truly how life should be lived when confronted with the difficulties and miseries of existence. Its exuberance rediscovers wondrous creation, hope, and realizes that God's goodness is infused into our bones. Our happiness becomes quite inseparable from Him. It is in this play that we are granted a preview of the magnificent union, the nuptial intimacy with our Bridegroom. Lewis's Christ-figure regains his strength after having risen from the dead. Before anything else, Aslan decides to play as no one has ever played before. The little brides and Bridegroom play chase, running in the high grass. They even play around the table of terrible sacrifice. Then the children and Aslan fall onto the warm and lush ground panting, but they are neither tired nor hungry nor thirsty. And why should they be? They are filled with everything because filled with Christ. Let us never forget that Christ entered existence as the unborn child and grew into his mission *through* childhood. His mother and father are the archetype of good and holy parents filled with love and joy. This is not a family without play, without gentleness wrapped in firmness and firmness wrapped in gentleness. This is the Holy Family, the most beautiful union of faith, redemptive suffering, love, and victory. Each power functions through play as openness to the heart of creation.

"Oh, children," said the Lion, "I feel my strength coming back to me. Oh, children, catch me if you can!" He stood for a second, his eyes very bright, his limbs quivering, lashing himself with his tail. Then he made a leap high over their heads and landed on the other side of the Table. Laughing, though she didn't know why, Lucy scrambled over it to reach him. Aslan leaped again. A mad chase began. Round and round the hill-top he led them, now hopelessly out of their reach, now letting them almost catch his tail, now diving between them, now tossing them in the air with his huge and beautifully velveted paws and catching them again, and now stopping unexpectedly so that all three of them rolled over together in a happy laughing heap of fur and arms and legs. It was such a romp as no one ever had except in Narnia; and whether it was more like playing with a thunderstorm or playing with a kitten Lucy could never make up her mind. And the funny thing was that when all three finally lay together panting in the sun, the girls no longer felt in the least tired or hunger or thirsty.
—C. S. Lewis, *The Lion the Witch and the Wardrobe*

The Lion Lays Down with the Lamb: What about Our Pets?

The wolf will live with the lamb, the leopard will lie down with the goat, the calf and the lion and the yearling together; and a little child will lead them.
—Isaiah 11:6

Paradise does not function as a repeat for earth. Just as earth is no recycling of Eden. If the fallen were somehow granted access inside the gates of Eden and able to survey the wondrous landscape, we would almost be a different species than Adam and Eve. Adam and Eve would raise their eyes, and as they walk, each movement is an easy, natural communication with the Divine. Each of the senses would experience the purely given, unfettered, unending life that surrounds them. They would exteriorize and interiorize the beauty of creation with each breath. We who have knowledge of good and evil and are filled with deteriorating worldly wisdom, fragmenting our senses, we would be unable to experience the garden as they do. They are fully liberated from death and disorder in all experience. We are not. Our glimpse of the resurrected state must not be confused with the comforts *well within* imagining. In every exile we lose something. Even if we gain the gift of immeasurable excellence, Christ, we cannot ignore that something has changed, has vanished, and is no longer present as it was. Christ overcomes death not by returning us to the garden but by making death the very vestment of eternal life. He wears that death, now overcome in His glorified body, rising with His scars.

Let us keep this truth of exile and redemption in mind when confronting powerful arguments against the return of our animals in the resurrected state. For Aquinas, if animals and plants are in the resurrected state, what form, if any, *could* they take? For animals to rise again it would be in the same manner as us. But they do not have immortal souls and their bodies after death go to nothing. Grace perfects nature, it needs a natural foundation to grow from. What can God work with if there is nothing left to the animal? Whatever remains in the world after it has been renewed will remain forever. But animals and plants are defined by birth and death. Therefore, they will cease after the resurrection. Aquinas's rationale falls well within the intelligible rejection of biological powers in paradise. We no longer need to eat to live, and there will be no new people, so procreation is not present in paradise. Should the highest actions within and defining these creatures be bound to such powers, then heaven is not their proper and final home. We are spiritual beings, a union of body and intellectual soul. We are not fulfilled with any natural or material end. But animals, including our beloved pets, are natural beings, each fulfilled and completed in a natural end. We are far closer to the angels than to the animals. This is due to our participation in God's image and likeness. This image in God is reserved only for humans and angels. It reflects our intellectual and transcendent natures. Our likeness differs from creatures that *only* possess likeness to God. Rather than it being a closed and static likeness, ours is in dialogue with image. Again, our likeness is a power that places us relatively above the angels.

Aquinas's stance is an important reminder of the necessity to shed earthly attachments until we embrace Christ. We must learn the painful, transformative lesson of redemption. We do not recover the home we lost when sin exiled us. Our exile is of such a sort that any return is impossible. Our sin collapsed our former home into dust and rubble. We do not repeat the comforts of earth. Salvation never works by repetition. There has never been an exact repeat of the past. Every political and theological effort is a shadow of what it tries to copy. God, in His perfection, never commits this error of errors. He knows better than any of us the consequences and effects of our freedom. Our free choices have a finality to them. Thus, if there is a place for our pets in paradise, it must be meaningful and a viable option. It cannot be that we fear losing our earthly comforts which reduces Paradise to irrelevance. Heaven is the foundation; it is no mere replication of earth.

In the tradition of St. Thomas Aquinas's writings, perhaps there is room for our own "on the contrary," which can demonstrate a potential path for our animals in the resurrected state. And here is the issue—the *resurrected* state. Heaven, and its state of the separated soul, make it difficult to manage some rationale for the pets' participation. The souls of animals are wholly bound to their bodies. But it is quite another to wonder about the architecture and scenery of the resurrection. We have stressed the likeness and especially the *difference* between ourselves and angels in terms of what reflects our state of perfection. We emphasized the unity of the body and soul and the contributions of the senses in our glorified bodies. When Christ resurrected on the third day, He was able to be heard, seen, and touched. He was made of flesh and blood, and He walked, talked, and moved in a world of time and space.

To have a body means to take up space, to be in contact with other things that take up space, which have length, breadth, texture, contour, are active and inert. A body means being in a world. All bodies are in a world. We are intellectual souls united to bodies. This means that we are uniquely world-forming creatures. We create homes, cities, friendships, make stories and love. The resurrected state could not be a blank room, a vacuum of nothingness, nor is it a mere mental state of relation. Grace perfects nature. If we are world-forming on earth, how much more fulfilled is our co-creation of the architecture of paradise? We participate in the architecture of paradise through Christ's flesh and blood identical with heaven. We are always taking in the beloved and interiorizing and exteriorizing ourselves repeatedly throughout our lives. A resurrection of an isolated person, really a shell of a person, appears to be the very antithesis of the incarnation. A world of beings coexists with all our actions. To claim that we resurrect with our bodies but there is no world to engage in appears to be contradictory. At present, we see through the glass darkly. We can wager that it makes far more sense that we resurrect with animals, plants, trees, places, and things. They are intrinsically bound up in the experience of our bodies, the world, and relationships.

The grandmother so very loved is housed in the memory of another in a different way. For her own grandparents, she is the little girl in a petticoat watching the farm animals out the train window during the Great War. She is in every way and in every age in others. Sometimes she is in the brick red colored jacket, the gloves pulled off for Mass, a moving form of strength equaled only by an incarnate shyness. Life is constructed by memory. Paradise is the hope of recovering what is lost. So many memories. Memory needs a foundation beyond the past image. It craves the scent and sound and the sight that blinds and blushes. And it seeks to be liberated from the painful yoke of recollection which can never quite recall what once was. In memory we are learning to forget under the guise of remembering what never quite was. Memory never lets us remember *as is*. The age or ages we are in heaven cannot be a single number but conjures a whole world of meaning and nuance that demands humility and attention.

> Then I saw "a new heaven and a new earth," for the first heaven and the first earth had passed away, and there was no longer any sea. I saw the Holy City, the new Jerusalem, coming down out of heaven from God, prepared as a bride beautifully dressed for her husband. And I heard a loud voice from the throne saying, "Look! God's dwelling place is now among the people, and he will dwell with them."
> —Revelation 21:1–3

We cannot know how things make it to paradise. We cannot make it on our own even if our souls are made divine. We cannot know how or if our pets, memories, and even the objects that illuminate our lives are to be participants in the afterlife. How would they appear in paradise? Resurrection is not a repeat of earth. Still, because of the Love that overflows, uniting these things to us, it appears more likely that they are present in a transformed vitality in paradise. Also, if we are to resurrect, why would there be a world of things and beings unattached to our sanctity? And unattached to our lives that first brought us to the promise of eternal life? Our own "on the contrary" points out three paths for our animals. These points are even for the things whose created goodness assisted in bringing us into the hearth of divinity:

1. Distinct from the state of the separated soul, the resurrected state means a body, and a body means a world. A world means an abundance of creatures and things.

2. Our natures are world-forming. We are always interiorizing and exteriorizing ourselves and others. This means that who we are is always beyond ourselves and within the world. How then does it do justice

to our natures, if that world of us is quashed in paradise? Such a state seems more the disintegration in hell.

3. If we concede that the resurrection means a new world for the bride, a *"new heaven and a new earth,"* filled with the waters of life, and the city we co-substantiate through Christ's flesh and blood can only be described poetically with the most precious of jewels, *"the foundations of the city walls were decorated with every kind of precious stone,"* why would this co-creation be wholly alien to our memories and longer way or to Christ's, who was born of woman?

Humans impart onto their pets a certain imprint of their selfhood. If the human person achieves salvific immortality, then in turn might the animal companion, who has taken on this *self*, receive this gift as well? If God raises us up and the world we have interiorized and exteriorized, then couldn't our pets receive a derivative immortality in the process? We can also say that such animals are worthy, in a way, of this derivative immortality. Our pets first invoked in us the gentle, playful otherness needed to achieve a holy, loving, and selfless personhood. If we know ourselves only in relation to others, can we appropriately envision a heaven without this animal-and-human relationship? This union cultivates the often gentler and kinder vision of ourselves than the diminished versions we receive and impart through our corrupted states.

> But ask the animals, and they will teach you, or the birds in the sky, and they will tell you; or speak to the earth, and it will teach you, or let the fish in the sea inform you. Which of all these does not know that the hand of the LORD has done this? In his hand is the life of every creature and the breath of all mankind.
> —Job 12:7–10

In Genesis, the earth began in the mystery of the garden. It was filled with creatures foreshadowing the animals around the manger, each longing for the new earth. How can this "new earth" of the resurrection be void of that life? St. Paul, who speaks of heaven as home, states that *"creation itself would be set free from slavery to corruption and share in the glorious freedom of the children of God."* This implies a new world, not a void or a wasteland or a mind-only relationship. What is sought in the resurrected state is something sensed in play and in animal kinship. It is the reality of love touching all things, even the most disfigured, and transfiguring them with beauty and untroubled peace working wholly within God's intent:

Brothers, have no fear of men's sin. Love a man even in his sin, for that is the semblance of Divine Love and is the highest love on Earth. Love all God's creation, the whole and every grain of sand in it. Love every leaf, every ray of God's light. Love the animals, love the plants, love everything. If you love everything, you will perceive the divine mystery in things. Once you perceive it, you will begin to comprehend it better every day. And you will come at last to love the whole world with an all-embracing love. Love the animals: God has given them the rudiments of thought and joy untroubled. Do not trouble it, don't harass them, don't deprive them of their happiness, don't work against God's intent. Man, do not pride yourself on superiority to the animals; they are without sin, and you, with your greatness, defile the Earth by your appearance on it, and leave the traces of your foulness after you—alas, it is true of almost every one of us! Love children especially, for they too are sinless like the angels; they live to soften and purify our hearts and, as it were, to guide us. Woe to him who offends a child!
—Fyodor Dostoevsky, *The Brothers Karamazov*

The Mystery in Brief: Recovering Friendships and Intimacies

Fellowship is the most visible manifestation of our longer way to paradise. God is Love, and virtuous unions enable us to see with the eyes of Christ. True intimacy and friendliness are the spiritual dowries predisposing us to our union with the beatific vision. They are a central facet of the heavenly city. Through Christ, they form the very architecture of paradise. Friendship in Christ, as fellowship with the blessed, enables us to co-create heaven's rooms, valleys, corridors, and waters. Paradise would never be people separate and alone. How can praise of God and the beatific vision be inexhaustibly rich if the community is not truly *in* communion? How can the blessed be enjoined in praise if they do not love the Divine in others? We seek to discover *all* there is to love in others. This is the very essence of friendship, fulfilled in being a friend of God. And with Aristotle, *"Without friends, no one would want to live, even if he had all other goods."* Paradise without intimacy is an oxymoron, a contradiction in terms.

Now, to be sure, we recognize that intimacies must take on a dramatic excellence in paradise. It is a different and purer experience than many, if not most, friendships and bonds on earth. Like all worldly human actions, no friendship ever fully escapes the deadening grip of original sin. Vice has infected and wounded all things. Our sinfulness malforms friendships with its parasitical, unexamined, and failed loves, which separate what cannot be separated: intimacy and virtue. In paradise, the substance of friendship is to desire Christ for the beloved. And with equal and even greater zeal than one desires Christ for Himself. Intimacies and bonds within the fallen world dispose us to many substitutes and surrogates for genuine fellowship. We saw this in *Long Day's Journey into Night*. It prompts us to wonder: what happens to those partial forms, where there is a degree of authentic friendship but which fails to exercise its virtue? What becomes of the person who stubbornly refuses God but by his actions, or even despite them, has helped another along the way to salvation? We hope and pray there is a way through Christ. A good life lived must always sense the trembling mystery of our only true home. To experience the glimmer of heaven on earth, it is essential that it is won through the longer way of suffering, compassion, and self-emptying love. We must live with this mystery and love with a furiousness enlightened by the virtuous.

How are we to reconcile the summit of joy with the sight of the eternally diminished, alienated soul? If so many of our earthly friendships involve a range of allegiances and relationalities that distract us from salvation, what remains of those original friendships in the resurrected state? Are they simply unrecognizable, do we start over? Again, each of these questions reveals the most serious of mysteries: the potential total loss of Love itself. Hell is a possibility for any free being, but the church has never named anyone to hell and many to heaven. We can *only* know that this painful mystery beckons us here and now to love as truly and intensively as possible. To love with all the zeal of the virtues formed through the compassion Christ offers us. And it is through this endlessly relentless love alone that we tremble, glimpsing that sight of heaven incarnated within each of us. We are always straddling that delicate line. We must never envision heaven as a reductive extension of earth. We must practice, through to our death, the act of letting go all that is dear. And recognize that paradise must deeply reflect and exceed all our human conceptions of what it is to be flesh and blood, to be of earth and clay and spirit, to be world-forming and in the image of our Dear Christ.

> Her heart felt as if it were breaking in her breast, bleeding, and bleeding, young and fierce. From grief over the warm and ardent love which she had lost and still secretly mourned; from anguished joy over the pale, luminous love which drew her to the farthest

boundaries of life on this Earth. Through the great darkness that would come, she saw the gleam of another, gentler sun, and she sensed the fragrance of the herbs in the garden at world's end.
—Sigrid Undset, *Kristin Lavransdatter II: The Wife*

Guardian Angels, by Carol Scott

On the last day I feel the sky hurtling its heavens, Its cobalts and sapphires
Every time I had loved the sky, loved the sea, fallen deep into the sleep of you
All compressed into one on the last day, in the last hour
I put my feet down into the sand, time itself collecting me, repaying my fines
Foreshadowing resignation and sleep, the great dissolution, the eternal dissolve
Which only God can re-collect on the last hour
In the last moment before I lose my name, I hope it is your name on my lips
Breathing you in, breathing you out, each syllable particulate matter
Finery, drawn lace, long sighs of you, as if your name is an angel
Your name guiding me in that last moment, when all the pain, all the pandering
All the pleading bleeds out, sinks the sun below the earth, my mind below memory
My children, the smell of their heads, their pretty little faces, just the thought
Solidifying my blood, stopping my heart, the mere sight of them inside me
Roads that dip, cold drink, cool sip, Autumn waiting for winter
The passion of you, all bound up, these things, the perfumes of my life
The sex, the sweat, the water, the wine, the pressed oil, scooped out avocado
Delicious sweet cream, risen steam, you watching me cook, watching me make a mess
I am watching you sleep, you fall asleep too easily, the curve of you, dreaming bow at your gates
To drink at your well, the sound of your voice, long sighs of you, as if your name is an angel
Guiding me, the sound of you, spoken through mine
In the last moment

    — "On the Way," by Caitlin Smith Gilson

Bibliography

Aeschylus, Sophocles, and Euripides. *The Greek Plays: Sixteen Plays by Aeschylus, Sophocles, and Euripides*. Translated by Mary Lefkowitz and James Romm. New York: Modern Library, 2017.
Ambrose. *The Letters of St. Ambrose, Bishop of Milan*. Translated by Henry Walford. Oxford: James Parker, 1881.
Anselm. *The Devotions of St. Anselm*. Edited by C. C. J. Webb. London: Methuen, 1903.
Aquinas, Thomas. *De Veritate*. Translated by Robert W. Mulligan. Chicago: Regnery, 1952.
———. *In Librum Beati Dionysii de Divinis Nominibus Expositio*. Edited by C. Pera and C. Mazzantini. Turin: Marietti, 1950.
———. *Meditations for Lent*. Translated by Philip Hughes. London: Sheed & Ward, 1937.
———. *On Being and Essence (De Ente et Essentia)*. Translated by Armand Maurer. Toronto: Pontifical Institute of Mediaeval Studies, 1949.
———. *Summa Contra Gentiles*. Translated by James F. Anderson. South Bend, IN: University of Notre Dame Press, 1992.
———. *Summa Theologiae*. Edited by Thomas Gilby. New York: Cambridge University Press, 1967.
Aristotle. *The Basic Works of Aristotle*. Edited by R. McKeon. New York: Random House, 1941.
Augustine. *City of God*. Edited by Vernon Bourke. New York: Image, 1958.
———. *Confessions*. Translated by Henry Chadwick. New York: Oxford University Press, 1998.
Balthasar, Hans Urs von. *The Christian and Anxiety*. San Francisco: Ignatius, 2000.
———. *Dare We Hope That All Men Be Saved? With a Short Discourse on Hell*. San Francisco: Ignatius, 2014.
———. *Love Alone Is Credible*. Translated by D. C. Schindler. San Francisco: Ignatius, 2004.
———. *Theo-Logic II: Truth of God*. San Francisco: Ignatius, 1994.
Behr, John. *The Mystery of Christ: Life in Death*. Yonkers, NY: St Vladimir's Seminary Press, 2006.
Belloc, Hilaire. *A Conversation with an Angel: And Other Essays*. New York: Harper, 1929.
———. "Dedicatory Ode." In *Verses*. London: Duckworth, 1910.
———. *The Path to Rome*. London: Allen & Unwin, 1916.
Benedict XVI. *Deus Caritas Est*. Vatican City: Libreria Editrice Vaticana, 2005.
Bernard of Clairvaux. *Bernard of Clairvaux: Selected Works*. Translated by Gillian Rosemary Evans. New York: Paulist, 1987.

Bibliography

Blot, François René. *In Heaven We'll Meet Again: The Saints and Scriptures on Our Heavenly Reunion*. Manchester: Sophia Institute, 2016.

Callard, Agnes. "The Philosophy of Anger." *Boston Review* 45.1 (2020) 9.

Camus, Albert. *Caligula and Three Other Plays*. Translated by Stuart Gilbert. New York: Vintage, 1962.

Catholic Church. *Catechism of the Catholic Church*. Vatican City: Libreria Editrice Vaticana, 2000.

———. *The Office for the Dead: According to the Roman Breviary, Missal and Ritual*. Toronto: Gale, 2010.

Chekhov, Anton. *The Lady with the Little Dog and Other Stories, 1896–1904*. Translated by Ronald Wilks. London: Penguin, 2002.

Chesterton, Gilbert Keith. *Heretics, Orthodoxy, the Blatchford Controversies*. Vol. 1 of *The Collected Works of G. K. Chesterton*. San Francisco: Ignatius, 1986.

———. *The Everlasting Man*. San Francisco: Ignatius, 1993.

———. "Jesus or Christ." *Hibbert Journal* (1909) 746–58.

———. *A Miscellany of Men*. New York: Dodd, Mead, and Company, 1912.

Coleridge, Samuel Taylor. *Kubla Kahn*. In *Samuel Taylor Coleridge: The Major Works*, edited by H. J. Jackson. Oxford: Oxford University Press, 2009.

Cummings, Edward Estlin. "Somewhere I Have Never Travelled." In *100 Selected Poems*. New York: Grove, 1994.

Dante Alighieri. *The Divine Comedy: The Inferno, the Purgatorio, and the Paradiso*. Translated by John Ciardi. New York: NAL Trade, 2003.

———. *La Vita Nuova*. Translated by David Slavitt. Cambridge: Harvard University Press, 2010.

Debout, Jacques. *My Sins of Omission*. Translated by J. F. Scanlan. London: Sands, 1930.

Derrida, Jacques. *The Gift of Death*. Translated by David Wills. Chicago: University of Chicago Press, 1995.

Desmond, William. *The Gift of Beauty and the Passion of Being: On the Threshold between the Aesthetic and the Religious*. Veritas. Eugene, OR: Cascade, 2018.

Dostoevsky, Fyodor. *The Brothers Karamazov*. Translated by Richard Pevear and Larissa Volokhonsky. New York: Farrar, Straus, and Giroux. 1990.

Eliot, T. S. *Collected Poems, 1909–1962*. Orlando: Harcourt, 1991.

Engelland, Chad. *Phenomenology*. Cambridge: MIT Press, 2020.

Francis. "Gaudete et Exsultate." Vatican City: Libreria Editrice Vaticana, 2018.

———. "Laudato Si." Vatican City: Libreria Editrice Vaticana, 2015."

Gilson, Caitlin Smith. *Immediacy and Meaning: J. K. Huysmans and the Immemorial Origin of Metaphysics*. London: Bloomsbury, 2018.

———. *Metaphysical Presuppositions of Being-in-the-World: A Confrontation between St. Thomas Aquinas and Martin Heidegger*. New York: Continuum, 2010.

———. *The Philosophical Question of Christ*. London: Bloomsbury, 2014.

———. *The Political Dialogue of Nature and Grace: Toward a Phenomenology of Chaste Anarchism*. London: Bloomsbury, 2015.

———. *Subordinated Ethics: Natural Law and Moral Miscellany in Aquinas and Dostoyevsky*. Eugene, OR: Cascade, 2020.

Gilson, Étienne. *The Elements of Christian Philosophy*. New York: Mentor Omega, 1963.

Girard, René. *Things Hidden Since the Foundation of the World*. Translated by Stephen Bann and Michael Metteer. Stanford, CA: Stanford University Press, 1987.

———. *Violence and the Sacred*. Translated by Patrick Gregory. Baltimore: Johns Hopkins University, 1979.
Guardini, Romano. *Pascal for Our Time*. Translated by Brian Thompson. New York: Herder, 1966.
Haydock, George Leo, ed. *The Douay-Rheims New Testament of Our Lord and Savior Jesus Christ*. Monrovia, Liberia: Catholic Treasures, 1991.
———. *The Douay-Rheims Old Testament of the Holy Catholic Bible*. Monrovia, Liberia: Catholic Treasures, 1992.
Heidegger, Martin. *The Phenomenology of Religious Life*. Translated by Matthias Fritsch and Jennifer Anna Gosetti-Ferenci. Bloomington: Indiana University Press, 2010.
———. *Poetry, Language, Thought*. Translated by Albert Hofstadter. New York: Harper & Row, 1971.
Hugo, Victor. "La Conscience." In *La Légende des Siècles*. Translated by Dublin University Magazine. Online. https://www.gutenberg.org/files/8775/8775-h/8775-h.htm.
Huizinga, Johan. *The Waning of the Middle Ages*. Mineola, NY: Dover, 2013.
Huysmans, Joris Karl. *The Damned (Là-Bas)*. Translated by T. Hale. London: Penguin, 2001.
———. *The Oblate*. Translated by Edward Perceval. London: Kegan Paul, 1918.
Jaeger, Werner. *Theology of the Early Greek Philosophers*. New York: Oxford University Press, 1947.
Jaspers, Karl. *Philosophical Faith and Revelation*. Translated by E. B. Ashton. New York: Harper & Row, 1967.
John of the Cross. *The Collected Works of St. John of the Cross*. Translated by Kieran Kavanaugh and Otilio Rodriguez. Washington, DC: ICS, 1991.
———. *A Spiritual Canticle of the Soul and the Bride Christ*. Translated by David Lewis. Grand Rapids: Christian Classics Ethereal Library, 2000.
John Paul II. *Apostolic Letter Salvifici Doloris*. Vatican City: Libreria Editrice Vaticana, 1984.
Journet, Charles. *The Meaning of Grace*. Glen Rock, NJ: Paulist, 1962.
Julian of Norwich. *Revelations of Divine Love: Short Text and Long Text*. Translated by Elizabeth Spearing. London: Penguin, 1988.
Kierkegaard, Søren. *The Essential Kierkegaard*. Edited by Howard V. Hong and Edna. H. Hong. Princeton, NJ: Princeton University Press, 2000.
———. *Works of Love*. Translated by Howard V. Hong and Edna H. Hong. New York: Harper, 2009.
Kreeft, Peter. *Everything You Wanted to Know About Heaven but Never Dreamed of Asking*. San Francisco: Ignatius, 1990.
Levinas, Emmanuel. *Emmanuel Levinas: Basic Philosophical Writings*. Edited by Adriaan T. Peperzak et al. Bloomington: Indiana University Press, 1996.
Lewis, C. S. *The Abolition of Man*. New York: Harper, 2001.
———. *C. S. Lewis Signature Classics: Mere Christianity, The Screwtape Letters, A Grief Observed, The Problem of Pain, Miracles, and The Great Divorce*. New York: Harper, 2001.
———. *The Chronicles of Narnia*. New York: Harper, 2004.
———. *The Four Loves*. New York: Harper, 2001.
———. *A Grief Observed*. New York: Harper, 2001.
———. *Till We Have Faces: A Myth Retold*. New York: Harper, 1984.
———. *The Weight of Glory and Other Addresses*. New York: Harper, 2001.

Bibliography

Lubac, Henri de. *Catholicism: Christ and the Common Destiny of Man*. Translated by Lancelot C. Sheppard and Elizabeth Englund. San Francisco: Ignatius, 1988.

———. *The Drama of Atheistic Humanism*. Translated by Mark Sebanc. San Francisco: Ignatius, 1995.

Marion, Jean Luc. *God without Being*. Chicago: University of Chicago Press, 1995.

Maritain, Jacques. *Approaches to God*. Translated by Peter O'Reilly. New York: Harper, 1954.

———. *God and the Permission of Evil*. Translated by Joseph W. Evans. Milwaukee: Bruce, 1966.

———. *The Grace and Humanity of Jesus Christ*. Translated by Joseph W. Evans. New York: Herder & Herder, 1969.

———. *The Peasant of the Garonne: An Old Layman Questions Himself About the Present Time*. Translated by Michael Cuddihy and Elizabeth Hughes. Reprint, Eugene, OR: Wipf & Stock, 2013.

Mauriac, Francois. *The Inner Presence: Recollection of My Spiritual Life*. Indianapolis: Bobbs-Merrill, 1968.

Meister Eckhart. *Breakthrough: Meister Eckhart's Creation Spirituality in New Translation*. Translated by Matthew Fox. Garden City, NY: Image, 1980.

Merleau-Ponty, Maurice. *The Phenomenology of Perception*. Translated by Donald A. Landes. New York: Routledge, 2013.

Milton, John. *Paradise Lost*. Edited by Roy C. Flannagan. New York: Dover, 2005.

Newman, John Henry. *The Apologia Pro Vita Sua*. New York: Norton, 1968.

———. *Meditations and Devotions*. London: Longmans, 1933.

Nietzsche, Friedrich. *Basic Writings*. Translated by Walter Kaufmann. New York: Modern Library, 2000.

Nussbaum, Martha. *Anger and Forgiveness: Resentment, Generosity, Justice*. Oxford: Oxford University Press, 2016.

O'Connor, Flannery. *The Habit of Being*. New York: Farrar, Straus and Giroux, 1988.

———. *A Prayer Journal*. Edited by W. A. Sessions. New York: Farrar, Straus, and Giroux, 2013.

O'Regan, Cyril. *The Anatomy of Misremembering*. New York: Herder, 2014.

———. *Theology and the Spaces Apocalyptic*. Milwaukee: Marquette University Press, 2009.

Pascal, Blaise. *Pensees*. Translated by William Finlayson Trotter. New York: Dutton, 1958.

Pegis, Anton Charles. *At the Origins of the Thomistic Notion of Man*. New York: Macmillan, 1963.

———. *The Problem of the Soul in the Thirteenth Century*. Toronto: Pontifical Institute of Mediaeval Studies, 1934.

Péguy, Charles. *God Speaks: Religious Poetry*. Translated by Julian Green. New York: Pantheon, 1945.

———. "I Am Their Father." In *Basic Verities*, translated by Ann Green and Julian Green. New York: Pantheon, 1943.

———. *Man and Saints*. Translated by Julian Green. New York: Pantheon, 1944.

———. *The Mystery of the Holy Innocents and Other Poems*. Translated by Pansy Pakenham. Reprint, Eugene, OR: Wipf & Stock, 2018.

———. *Notre Patrie*. Paris: Payen, 1905.

———. *The Portal of the Mystery of Hope*. Translated by David L. Schindler Jr. Grand Rapids: Eerdmans, 1996.

———. *Temporal and Eternal*. Translated by Alexandre Dru. Indianapolis: Liberty Fund, 2001.
Pieper, Josef. *Death and Immortality*. Translated by Richard Winston and Clara Winston. South Bend, IN: St. Augustine, 2000.
———. *Happiness and Contemplation*. South Bend, IN: St. Augustine, 1998.
Plato. *The Collected Dialogues of Plato, Including the Letters*. Edited by Edith Hamilton and Huntington Cairns. New York: Pantheon, 1961.
Pseudo-Dionysius. *The Complete Works*. Translated by Paul Rorem. Glen Rock, NJ: Paulist, 1987.
Rahner, Hugo. *Man at Play*. New York: Herder, 1967.
Rand, Ayn. *Atlas Shrugged*. Translated by Leonard Peikoff. New York: Penguin, 2005.
Ratzinger, Joseph. *On Conscience*. San Francisco: Ignatius, 2007.
Rilke, Rainier Maria. *The Book of Hours: Prayers to a Lowly God*. Translated by Annemarie Kidder. Evanston, IL: Northwestern University Press, 2001.
———. *The Complete French Poems*. Translated by A. Poulin Jr. Saint Paul, MN: Graywolf, 2002.
———. *The Dark Interval: Letters on Loss, Grief, and Transformation*. Translated by Ulrich Baer. New York: Modern Library, 2018.
———. *The Duino Elegies*. Translated by Stephen Cohn. Evanston, IL: Northwestern University Press, 1989.
———. *Sonnets to Orpheus*. Translated by David Young. Hanover, NH: University Press of New England, 1987.
Santayana, George. *The Idea of Christ in the Gospels: Or God in Man, A Critical Essay*. New York: Scribner, 1946.
———. *Soliloquies in England and Later Soliloquies*. Ann Arbor: University of Michigan, 1967.
Sartre, Jean-Paul. *No Exit and Three Other Plays*. Translated by Stuart Gilbert. New York: Vintage, 1989.
Schindler, D. C. "Love and Beauty, the 'Forgotten Transcendental,' in Thomas Aquinas." *Communio* 44.2 (2017) 334–56.
Shakespeare, William. *The Complete Works of William Shakespeare*. Ware, UK: Wordsworth, 1996.
Shestov, Lev. *All Things Are Possible (Apotheosis of Groundlessness)*. Translated by Samuel Solomonovitch Kotelianksy. New York: McBride, 1920.
Solovyov, Vladimir. *The Meaning of Love*. Translated by Thomas R. Beyer. Hudson, NY: Lindisfarne, 1985.
Solzhenitsyn, Aleksandr. *The Gulag Archipelago: An Experiment in Literary Investigation*. Translated by Thomas P. Whitney. New York: Harper Collins, 1974.
Stein, Edith. *The Science of the Cross*. Translated by Josephine Koeppel. Washington, DC: ICS, 2002.
Steptoe, Andrew. *The Mozart-Da Ponte Operas: The Cultural and Musical Background to Le Nozze di Figaro, Don Giovanni, and Così fan Tutte*. Oxford: Oxford University Press, 1988.
Tennyson, Alfred. *In Memoriam*. London: Macmillan, 1906.
Teresa of Avila. *The Collected Works of St. Teresa of Avila*. Translated by Kieran Kavanaugh and Otilio Rodriguez. 2 vols. Washington, DC: ICS, 1976, 1980.
Tertullian. *Tertullian's Treatise on the Incarnation De Carne Christi*. Edited by Ernest Evans. London: SPCK, 1956.

Bibliography

Tolkien, J. R. R. *The Letters of J. R. R. Tolkien*. Edited by Christopher Humphries. New York: Houghton Mifflin Harcourt, 2000.

Traherne, Thomas. *Centuries of Meditations*. Edited by Bertram Dobell. London: Dobell, 1908.

Unamuno, Miguel. *Our Lord Don Quixote: The Life of Don Quixote and Sancho with Related Essays*. Translated by Anthony Kerrigan. Princeton, NJ: Princeton University Press, 1967.

———. *Tragic Sense of Life*. Translated by J. E. Crawford Flitch. Mineola, NY: Dover, 1952.

———. *Treatise on the Love of God*. Translated by Nelson R. Orringer. Champaign, IL: University of Illinois Press, 2011.

Undset, Sigrid. *Kristin Lavransdatter II: The Wife*. Translated by Tiina Nunnally. New York: Penguin, 1999.

Vianney, John. *Little Catechism of the Cure of Ars*. Gastonia, NC: Tan, 1994.

Voegelin, Eric. *What Is History? And Other Late Unpublished Writings*. Edited by Thomas A. Hollweck and Paul Caringella. Vol. 28 of *Collected Works*. Columbia, MO: University of Missouri Press, 1990.

Von Hildebrand, Dietrich. *Man, Woman and the Meaning of Love: God's Plan for Love, Marriage, Intimacy, and the Family*. Bedford, NH: Sophia Institute, 2002.

Von Speyr, Adrienne. *Confession*. San Francisco: Ignatius, 1985.

———. *The Cross: Word and Sacrament*. Translated by Graham Harrison. San Francisco: Ignatius, 2018.

Waugh, Evelyn. *Brideshead Revisited*. New York: Back Bay, 2008.

Williams, Charles. *The Figure of Beatrice*. Berkeley: Apocryphile, 2005.

Williams, William Carlos. "The Widow's Lament in Springtime." In *The Collected Poems of William Carlos Williams, Vol. 1: 1909–1939*. New York: New Directions, 1991.

Yeats, William Butler. *The Collected Poems of W. B. Yeats*. Edited by Richard J. Finnernan. New York: Scribner, 1996.

Index

Abortion, 24, 151
Agape, 126, 155
Alighieri, Dante, xiii, 52
Ambrose, Saint, 103–4
Aquinas, Saint Thomas, 19, 45–46, 48, 52, 97, 118, 135, 161, 170–71
Aristotle, 174
Augustine, Saint, xiii, 119, 140, 153

Balthasar, Hans Urs von, 104
Behr, John, 105
Belloc, Hilaire, 150
Bernard of Clairvaux, Saint, 143
Boethius, 82

Chesterton, G.K., 40–41, 81
Christ, xi, xiii, 10, 15, 20–26, 30–32, 36, 39–41, 45, 55, 64–65, 69–72, 74, 76, 78, 80, 82, 89, 91, 100, 102–5, 113–14, 116, 119, 125–47, 150–64, 167–71, 174–75
Colossians, 72, 123
Conscience, 73–91
Corinthians, 21, 126, 129, 142, 146, 151

Deuteronomy, 113, 120
Dostoyevsky, Fyodor, 174

Engelland, Chad, 99
Eros, 126, 155, 163

Forgiveness, 53, 76, 80, 83, 86, 90, 125, 147
Francis of Assisi, Saint, 62, 69

Genesis, 112, 115, 117–18, 123, 173
Gift, xii, 6, 16–21, 26, 32–33, 39–40, 51–52
Gorgias, 77
Grace, xvii, 19, 25, 29, 32–33, 36, 39, 53–54, 58, 61, 91, 94, 112, 119, 123, 125, 130, 132, 136–37, 141, 143, 146, 151, 155–57, 159, 161, 163, 166–67, 170–71

Hebrews, 25, 32, 123
Hell, xiii, xiii, 25–26, 58, 71, 73–91, 105, 130, 158, 168, 173, 175
Horizon, 36, 48, 53, 60, 102, 112
Hugo, Victor, 75

Image and Likeness, 48, 52–55, 80, 83–84, 88–89, 98, 100, 102, 122, 27, 155, 170
Immediacy, 116, 121, 133
Incarnation, xiii, 21, 26, 29, 31, 36, 39–40, 70, 80, 133, 135, 147, 153, 156, 171
Infixion, 141
Isaiah, 12, 157, 169

Jeremiah, 60, 115
Jerome, Saint, 124
Job, 123–24, 173

Index

John, 15, 55, 71–72, 103, 115, 117, 119–20, 130, 144, 164
Julian of Norwich, 39, 91
Justice, 77, 172

Lewis, C.S., 18, 100–101, 141, 168–69
Longer way, 36, 52, 58, 100, 115, 121, 124, 129, 173–75
Luke, 70, 115, 123

Mark, 115, 117, 164
Martyrological, 109, 137
Matthew, 120, 125, 133, 137
Merleau-Ponty, 121
Metaphysics, 79–80
Mozart, Wolfgang Amadeus, 11
Mystical, 41, 71, 104–5, 139, 134, 159, 163
Myth, 40–41

Newman, John Henry, 25

Obedience, 55, 119–20, 128, 152, 167
O'Connor, Flannery,
O'Neill, Eugene, xi, 80, 82, 85–88, 90–91
Otherness, 173

Paradise, xii, 19, 24, 26, 31–33, 36–37, 41–42, 45, 69, 67, 69, 79, 86, 99–100, 102, 112, 117, 120, 127, 129, 133–35, 141–42, 144, 146–64, 167–75
Paul, Saint, 38, 60, 73, 104, 122, 124, 173
Péguy, Charles, 37, 62, 109, 114, 156, 161
Phenomenology, 99, 121
Pieper, Josef, 94

Plato, 162
Political, 19, 79, 105, 170
Proverbs, 33, 123, 168
Psalms, 4, 29, 57, 101, 113, 123, 127, 143–44, 167

Revelation, 72, 113, 117, 172
Rilke, Rainer Maria, 96
Romans, 103

Salvation, 103–4, 117, 126, 133–34, 137, 142, 151, 170, 173, 175
Sartre, Jean Paul, 78
Schlick, Moritz,
Socrates, 77, 84
Solzhenitsyn, Aleksandr, 83–84
Song of Songs, 108, 128, 143, 145, 155

Tennyson, Alfred, 72
Teresa of Avila, Saint, 43, 163
Theology of the Body, 41, 164
Tragedy, xi, xiii, 36, 32, 78, 80–81, 85, 90–91, 95, 116, 151, 159–60
Transcendent, xii, 19, 25–26, 31–32, 40, 47, 49, 60, 72, 81, 88, 96, 99–101, 105, 115–16, 122, 125, 127–28, 146, 153–54, 159–60, 163, 167, 170
Transubstantiation, 104, 126

Unamuno, Miguel, 160
Uncreated, 60, 116, 134, 153, 155

Virtue, 14, 40–41, 47, 54, 69, 77–78, 82, 88, 112, 118, 133, 132, 135, 152–55, 161, 167, 174–75

Xavier, St. Francis, 151–52

www.ingramcontent.com/pod-product-compliance
Lightning Source LLC
Chambersburg PA
CBHW061940220426
43662CB00012B/1971